the province of
JOY

the province of

JOY

praying with
Flannery O'Connor

a book of hours
with OCCASIONS FOR MEDITATION

ANGELA ALAIMO O'DONNELL

PARACLETE PRESS BREWSTER, MASSACHUSETTS

The Province of Joy: Praying with Flannery O'Connor

2012 First printing

Copyright © 2012 by Angela Alaimo O'Donnell

ISBN 978-1-55725-703-1

Scripture references are taken from the *New Revised Standard Version Bible*, copyright © 1989 by the Division of Education of the National Council of Churches of Christ in the U.S.A., and are used by permission. All rights reserved.

Library of Congress Cataloging-in-Publication Data

O'Donnell, Angela Alaimo.
  The province of joy : praying with Flannery O'Connor / by Angela Alaimo O'Donnell.
      p. cm.
  Includes bibliographical references.
  ISBN 978-1-55725-703-1 (trade pbk.)
  1.   Catholic Church—Prayers and devotions. 2.   Spiritual life--Catholic Church. 3.   O'Connor, Flannery—Religion. I. Title.
  BX2182.3.O36 2012
  242'.802—dc23   2012000668

10 9 8 7 6 5 4 3 2 1

Published by Paraclete Press
Brewster, Massachusetts
www.paracletepress.com

Printed in the United States of America

contents

occasions for meditation

FAVORED PRAYERS, POEMS & PROSE PASSAGES

the province of
JOY

introduction

IN SEARCH OF "THE PROVINCE OF JOY"
Praying with Flannery O'Connor

I say Prime in the morning and sometimes I say Compline at night. . . . I like parts of my prayers to stay the same and part to change. So many prayer books are so awful, but if you stick to the liturgy, you are safe.

(HB, 159–60) (SEE A NOTE ON SOURCES, PAGE 26)

On May 19, 1956, Flannery O'Connor sent a letter containing these words along with the gift of *A Short Breviary* to her friend and correspondent Elizabeth Hester (addressed in O'Connor's letters as "A"). In the course of nine years, the two women exchanged many letters in which they addressed essential questions of faith and doubt, shared key points gleaned from their spiritual reading, and described their faith practices. It is notable that, despite this rich context for discussion of the practice of prayer, rarely does O'Connor discuss her own prayer life. These brief remarks help to clarify this seeming omission. As a Catholic, accustomed to a very particular way of praying prescribed by the church, O'Connor's practice was simple and very much in keeping with her faith tradition. Also, traditional Catholics—

especially those who practiced the faith before Vatican II—
tended not to talk a great deal about prayer. The assumption
was that fellow Catholics would know the prayers and say them
(or not), and non-Catholics would likely not be interested.

With O'Connor's own words as caveat and epigraph, I offer
this collection of prayers and readings that bear the stamp
of Flannery O'Connor's religious practice and imagination.
While it is true that O'Connor was a lifelong Catholic who
believed in liturgical prayer, she was also an intellectual
(despite her humble assurances to the contrary), a searcher
who cut a broad swath through spiritual and theological texts
of every stamp. She picked up ideas about the need for prayer
and its many forms as practiced by others, saints and sinners
alike. This book attempts to bring together O'Connor's
relatively spare and simple practice with the richness of the
spiritual context within which she lived and out of which she
wrote. Each day's collection offers prayers from the Divine
Office that she would have said, psalms and biblical passages
for contemplation, and quotations from her writings for *lectio
divina*. It is an attempt to assemble from materials O'Connor
would have invested with authority and significance a prayer
book that she would not find "awful," but instead, might see
as a helpful guide for those seeking a language and format
for prayer that places ancient practice within a contemporary
context. It also provides an opportunity to engage the rich
theological imagination of Flannery O'Connor, to come
into daily contact with her special mode of holiness—one
that is grounded in her unswerving love for Christ and
characterized by her extraordinary clarity of vision and a
fearless commitment to her craft as a means of accomplishing
good in the world.

The Life and the Work

Flannery O'Connor is known to most literary-minded readers as one of the finest writers of twentieth-century American fiction. In addition, she is of particular interest to a growing number of readers who are interested in writers who consciously explore the intersection between art and faith.

Born in Savannah on March 25, 1925 (the Feast of the Annunciation, happily enough), she was christened Mary Flannery O'Connor by her parents, Regina Cline and Edward F. O'Connor, both observant Catholics. (She would later drop the "Mary" and use her middle name, instead, as a more fitting—and memorable—pen name for a novelist.) Flannery grew up an only child under their watchful eye, attending parochial school until the family moved to the small town of Milledgeville in 1938. There, she attended a small public laboratory school, associated with the Georgia State College for Women, where she would eventually pursue a bachelor's degree in social sciences. Her reasonably happy childhood, however, came to an end quite suddenly at age fifteen when her father died from lupus, a heredity disease which would, eventually, afflict Flannery and cause her own premature death at the age of thirty-nine.

Much affected by the loss of her father, O'Connor chose to remain close to home during her college years, but set out on her own in 1946 to attend graduate school at the prestigious Iowa Writer's Workshop. It was there that O'Connor's vocation as a writer became abundantly clear, both to her and to her classmates and mentors. She made important literary connections and found herself, a few months after earning her Master's degree in Fine Arts, pursuing her writing at the

Yaddo Writer's Colony in upstate New York and in New York City. Among O'Connor's friends and colleagues were a number of influential Catholic writers, including translator, poet, and professor Robert Fitzgerald and his wife, Sally. The kinship between O'Connor and the Fitzgeralds was deep, based as it was on their common faith and their common love of the written word as a means of exploring and expressing the truths of their faith. In 1949, O'Connor accepted an invitation to take up residence with the Fitzgerald family in Redding, Connecticut, a peaceful setting (even with the multiple Fitzgerald offspring), one she much preferred to the noise and busy-ness of New York.

In the winter of 1951, O'Connor began to notice lethargy and weakness in her arms. During her return visit to Georgia for the Christmas holidays, she saw the family physician and was diagnosed with lupus. In addition to discovering that she would have to bear the burden of the disease that killed her father, she learned that the treatments necessary to keep her alive would confine her to Georgia for the rest of her life, far from the rich literary and intellectual life she had cultivated and enjoyed for the previous five years. O'Connor would endure this exile gracefully and with good humor until her death on August 3, 1964. She would also continue her writing, despite the painful and debilitating effects of both the disease and the medications prescribed to remedy it. Against all odds, O'Connor would produce two novels, thirty-two short stories, and many essays, reviews, and commentaries in her thirteen years at Andalusia, the family farm where she lived with her mother. In addition, O'Connor became a prolific writer of letters—long, wonderful, old-fashioned letters, exchanged among friends but also with other writers and with readers who made her acquaintance through her work. This remarkable correspondence became an essential means for O'Connor to continue the rich intellectual and spiritual conversation she had grown accustomed to, and it is in these letters that readers discover the quality and strength of her faith, the complexity of her vision, and the passion she brought to her work and her life in the world.

The Province of Joy

In one of these letters, written on July 14, 1964, just three weeks before her death, O'Connor copied out "The Prayer of St. Raphael" and sent it to her friend Janet McKane. This laborious enterprise was the fulfillment of her promise to share her favorite prayer, one she said every day for many years. Nine years earlier, in a letter to another friend, O'Connor recounted her discovery of this prayer that would, ultimately, become part of her daily office. It had arrived in the mail printed on a card she received from the Catholic Worker. She paraphrased what was, to her, the key line: "The prayer asks St. Raphael to guide us to the province of joy so that we may not be ignorant of the concerns of our true country" (HB, 132).

This line is particularly poignant in light of the difficult circumstances of O'Connor's life. In the face of loneliness, isolation, daily physical pain and limitation, and the psychological burden of living with a fatal disease, her daily prayer to St. Raphael, "the Angel of Happy Meeting," is daily passage to the "province of joy." O'Connor knew that the "true country," the proper destination, orientation, and disposition of a believing Christian, is joy—a word with a rich history of theological nuance, suggesting as it does both heaven (a place toward which we tend) and paradise (the place where human beings originated). In both cases, joy is a place and circumstance that belongs to us.

Through prayer and through her writing, which served as a kind of prayer for O'Connor, she could place herself on the threshold of that province using the power of word and imagination. Prayer, for O'Connor, was a means of moving from the limited place in which she found herself toward the limitless space of joy, a location that can be occupied in the here and now, as well as looked forward to in eternity. Indeed, prayer becomes both means and end for all of us, an act that propels us toward the prospect of eternity and an experience of the eternal achieved, paradoxically, within the limits of time and physical space. Such prayer provides the pray-er with a foretaste of paradise. As poet Emily Dickinson writes, "Instead of getting to heaven at last / I'm going all along." Given the power of this prayer, in particular, it's no wonder O'Connor felt the need to share it with those dear to her, and we are fortunate to be recipients of this gift, as well.

Praying with Flannery O'Connor

This book of hours is unique in its focus on a Catholic laywoman who is known, primarily, as a fiction writer. However, readers familiar with O'Connor's stories know they are made up of a rich blend of theology and imagination. She is a writer who creates her art from the standpoint of belief and serves as an example of one who is both intellectually and imaginatively engaged and a faithful Christian. Furthermore, she sees no conflict between these identities. Quite the contrary, her faith informs her art, and her art helps to confirm her faith. Thus, many readers over the last half century have looked to O'Connor for spiritual guidance as well as to be delighted by her stories.

These daily prayers provide an opportunity for readers who are familiar with O'Connor's fiction to deepen their relationship to the spiritual life of its creator. They provide a glimpse into the sacred texts O'Connor knew well, the biblical stories that informed her salvific vision, and the daily language of prayer that inflects her narrative voice.

For those who are, as yet, unfamiliar with O'Connor's writings, this book of hours might serve as introduction to her novels and stories. The intimacy achieved through daily practice of her prayer habits and through meditation on excerpts from her letters and essays will provide, I hope, a foundation on which to build a relationship of even greater understanding and intimacy. While O'Connor is a fellow laborer in the Fields of the Lord, her special labor as a writer is a boon and a blessing to all of us. Her writing bodies forth and clarifies the central tenets of Christian faith bravely and brilliantly. Reading her stories is a means of becoming more fully engaged in the world, of seeing it more clearly, and of perceiving God's living presence among us in the most unexpected places.

PRIME AND COMPLINE

In keeping with O'Connor's personal spiritual practice, this prayer book offers a version of Prime and Compline— Morning and Evening Prayer—for each day of the week. The

order of the readings is based on the order of the Divine
Office, and some of the key prayers associated with Prime
and Compline are included as well. (More specific informa-
tion about the nature and ordering of these prayers appears
below.)

THEOLOGICAL THEMES

The Prime and Compline prayers are supplemented with
readings from the Gospels, the letters of the New Testament, and
the Psalms. Each day's readings are keyed to a theological theme,
one for each day of the week. The seven themes are rooted in
key Christian concepts that surface in O'Connor's writings with
some frequency and are expressed in the *lectio divina* passages
excerpted from O'Connor's work in both Morning and Evening
Prayer. These themes, along with a brief explanation of each, are
as follows:

SUNDAY: *The Christian Comedy*

The word *comedy* here is used in two senses. Most obviously,
comedy suggests a sense of humor, a disposition toward joy
and an appreciation of the play of paradox that governs human
affairs. O'Connor is known for her great sense of humor. As
a keen observer of human nature and of ordinary life, she is
aware of the fact that tragedy and comedy cannot be readily
separated, and her stories often set these seeming opposites side
by side.

In addition, the term *comedy* refers to the literary genre of
Comedy, wherein circumstances at the beginning of a play that
threaten impending disaster are reversed. Errors are corrected,
offenses are forgiven, and divisions are healed, bringing about
unity, amity, and general accord at the end of the drama, a

reunion often signified by a marriage celebration. Comedy asserts that Good can come of Evil, and thus serves as a fitting trope for Christian salvation history, wherein the divine plan for human happiness that *seems* to be ruined by the Fall of Adam and Eve ultimately unfolds, as a result of the redeeming power of the Incarnation. Comedy asserts that "nothing is impossible," and the Christian Comedy, in particular, asserts that "nothing is impossible with God." This trope has been used by many spiritual writers and poets, perhaps most famously by Dante in his great poem of salvation, *The Divine Comedy.* A comprehensive artistic and theological vision is one that takes this totality into account and sees that tragedy is unfinished comedy, to the Christian imagination.

MONDAY: *The False Self & the True Self*

O'Connor's characters are often good people who allow themselves to be distracted and misled by idols. Chief among the idols they fall victim to is a false sense of the self they fabricate and try to conform to. Some of her characters even go so far as to rename themselves as part of the effort to remake themselves. If they are fortunate—and open to the operation of grace—they are finally able to recognize the false self for what it is and make a genuine attempt to be the person God created them to be. What is true of O'Connor's characters is true of us all, to some extent. Monday's readings and prayers focus on the necessity of recognizing and shedding the false version of the self and embracing our true identity and purpose.

TUESDAY: *Blindness & Vision*

Another spiritual affliction O'Connor's characters suffer from is moral blindness—a sometimes willful refusal to recognize and embrace the good. One of the ways in which grace operates in her stories is as a sudden insight or vision occurring to a character, often precipitated, unfortunately, by some violent action or event. But once the person's vision is corrected, he or she finds him or herself in considerably less spiritual peril. Tuesday's readings invite us to ponder instances of this sudden sight among the saints and to contemplate the ways in which our own moral vision might benefit from correction.

WEDNESDAY: *Limitation & Grace*

As a sufferer of lupus, O'Connor knew firsthand about the ways in which suffering could serve as a spring of love and a means to grace. In her letters, she describes with patience, wit, and good humor the gradual diminishment of her physical capacity. Even as she approached her premature death, O'Connor poured herself into her stories (which were labors of love) and her letters (which were gifts to her friends). It comes as no surprise, then, that her stories are filled with characters who suffer physical, mental, and spiritual limitations—missing limbs, bad hearts, poor eyesight, mental retardation, deafness, and muteness—yet it is precisely these afflictions that lead to their salvation and the salvation of others. Wednesday's readings invite us into the sufferings of biblical men and women as a means of understanding our own.

THURSDAY: *The Mystery of Incarnation*

O'Connor's characters often find themselves confounded by the mystery that is at the center of the universe. Many of them have gone through life believing they understood themselves and the people around them, but once they begin to closely examine their presumptions, they experience the miraculous nature of the world, the presence of the supernatural in the natural, and are filled with awe that enables them to transcend their small and broken selves. Thursday's readings and prayers invite us to meditate on the grace of being embodied and on the imminent presence of the Divine that makes itself known to us through the senses. These prayers serve, in some ways, as a counterpoint to Wednesday's meditations, emphasizing as they do the physical as a means of transcending limitation.

FRIDAY: *Facing the Dragon*

O'Connor read the writings of St. Cyril of Jerusalem and was so struck by the following passage that she chose it as the epigraph to her short story collection *A Good Man Is Hard to Find*: "The dragon sits by the side of the road, watching those who pass. Beware lest he devour you. We go to the Father of Souls, but it is necessary to pass by the dragon." The dragon, who clearly serves as a metaphor for spiritual danger or temptation that waits for the individual soul, can take many forms, and does so in O'Connor's stories. The characters who recognize and do battle with the dragon are those who stand some chance of salvation, whereas those who do not—or those who actually serve as the dragon for others—are most likely to lose their souls. It seems appropriate to spend Friday—the day of the week traditionally associated with Christ's passion and death—contemplating this spiritual danger and praying for the courage to face our dragons when we, inevitably, encounter them.

SATURDAY: *Revelations & Resurrections*

O'Connor's characters who do manage to overcome their false selves, who achieve vision instead of blindness, whose limitations lead to grace, and who overcome the dragon, are rewarded with the revelation of God's presence in and love for the suffering world. It seems fitting to spend Saturday—the day and evening before the celebration of Sunday's graces and the cosmic Comedy of the Resurrection—contemplating the ways in which God reveals himself to his followers.

Morning Prayer (Prime)

Each day of Morning Prayer begins with a passage drawn from the Gospels that engages the theological theme for the day followed by a brief silence during which the person praying can focus his or her mind and heart on these words and their possible meanings.

This is followed by the Invitatory from the Divine Office—the prayer said only once in the course of the day when one offers prayer for the first time—raising one's voice up to God.

This is followed by the psalm and the reading, both selected in keeping with the theological theme.

The *lectio divina* passage is excerpted from O'Connor's writings and provides an opportunity for the pray-er to consider the wisdom of theological observation in the context of prayer. Read the passage repeatedly as a means of understanding it in all of its tonality and complexity, then pause to reflect and meditate further upon its significance, particularly with regard to the prayers that surround it. A response to O'Connor's writing can vary greatly depending on the immediate context you bring to it. It also provides the opportunity for you to extend your sense of boundaries. O'Connor frequently uses humor, for example, to make serious theological points, and reading such observations in the midst of serious prayer ought not be dissonant, but instead affirming and joyful.

This meditation is followed by the Gospel Canticle, in keeping with the Divine Office (the Canticle of Zechariah in the morning and the Canticle of Mary—the Magnificat—in the evening). These prayers express joyful wonder at God's salvific plan.

Following these Canticles, you may insert intercessions as desired, concluding with the Lord's Prayer.

After these prayers of praise and petition comes a prayer of thanksgiving and reflection. I have composed each of these, attempting to bring together the themes of the readings, scriptural passages, psalms, and *lectio divina* with an eye toward the primary spiritual graces that are being highlighted.

Finally, Morning Prayer concludes with the aforementioned Prayer of St. Raphael, the Angel of Happy Meeting. This O'Connor said daily and shared with others in her letters. It is an excellent way to end Morning Prayer and to begin the day as it looks forward to the gifts the hours ahead might hold, particularly in the form of the people you might meet.

Following Morning Prayer—and Evening Prayer, as well—is a section for further reading and reflection. In this section I offer links and parallels between the themes, readings, and/or prayers of the day with O'Connor's fiction. These parallels are offered as illustration of some of the ways that O'Connor's practice of her faith and her art intersect and serve to illuminate one another. Those readers new to O'Connor's work who are interested in exploring the ways in which her fiction embodies Christian teaching and theological concepts might like to read the stories mentioned in light of the prayers of the day. For those readers already familiar with the stories and characters, these suggested parallels might afford new or further insights into O'Connor's rich and complex imaginative and theological vision.

Evening Prayer (Compline)

Prayer in the evening begins with the same Gospel meditation considered for Morning Prayer. (The only exception to this is Friday, wherein I choose to repeat the *lectio divina* rather than the Gospel meditation. This is one way to set Friday, the day traditionally associated with Christ's crucifixion, apart from the rest of the week. This is in keeping with traditional Friday observances, such as fasting and abstinence and First Friday masses.) The repetition of the Gospel meditation gives you the opportunity to revisit the theological theme at day's end and provides a sense of closure for the day.

Each day of Evening Prayer includes the recitation of a psalm, a reading, and a *lectio divina* passage (drawn, again, from O'Connor's writing) keyed to that day's theme.

After a brief meditation on O'Connor's words there is an opportunity to perform an examination of conscience, during which you consider the events of the day in the light of eternity. You may ask the questions: Where did I feel God's presence today in my own actions or those of others? Where did I feel God's absence? You may then frame your intercessions according to your own conscience and request the spiritual gifts you most need.

Evening prayer then concludes with the Canticle of Mary (the Magnificat), in keeping with the Divine Office, and also the Nunc Dimittis, which is generally the final prayer said before retiring.

The concluding lines ask for a peaceful sleep and a peaceful death, bringing time together with eternity, reminding us that our nightly sleep is a harbinger of the long sleep to come, just as the rising at morning is a harbinger of the resurrection.

Additional Readings and Prayers

In addition to this daily guide for prayer, the book includes a section titled, "Occasions for Meditation: Favored Prayers, Poems & Prose Passages." Here you will find intercessory prayers and sayings attributed to saints, each of which Flannery O'Connor felt some interest in and kinship with. These include passages from favorite books O'Connor reflected on and poems written by poets O'Connor recognized as kindred spiritual seekers. Many of these prayers, poems, and passages are excerpted from books that O'Connor owned and collected in her library at Andalusia. These were the books O'Connor read on a regular basis during her long exile, and many of them contain markings and marginalia indicating particular passages she wished to emphasize, return to, and remember. Many of the passages included in this section are those O'Connor marked. In addition, a number of these passages appear in her letters and essays, as she was moved to share them with friends, readers, and correspondents. These are offered as supplemental sources of meditation and contemplation to further enrich this encounter with O'Connor's deeply imaginative life of prayer.

A Note on Sources

Most of the quotations by Flannery O'Connor were drawn from O'Connor's collected letters, *The Habit of Being* (abbreviated HB). Others come from her essays and lectures collected in *Mystery and Manners* (abbreviated MM). These books offer great insight into O'Connor's thoughts, struggles, hopes, and fears, and enable us to enter into a sort of vicarious friendship with her. To those who enjoy the excerpted passages, as well as this method of prayer, I highly recommend reading these books in their entirety.

The scripture passages are drawn from the *New Revised Standard Version* (1989). This particular standard translation is widely known to most Christian readers and is suitably poetic to facilitate prayer. Finally, the prayers of the Divine Office are drawn from *The Liturgy of the Hours*.

Flannery, Thee, and Me

As a writer, poet, and longtime professor of English and American literature, I have been a great admirer of Flannery O'Connor's work for several decades. I am privileged to have read her writings long and deeply and to have taught her stories to thousands of students. One testimony to the richness of her writing is that despite my familiarity with the stories, they continue to open up and reveal new depths to me each time I reread and reteach them. Living with her work has only increased my appreciation and admiration for O'Connor as both an artistic visionary and a craftsman.

In addition to my respect for her gifts as a writer, I have immense admiration for O'Connor as a person of deep faith. Despite physical adversity, she was determined to practice her vocation as a Christian/Catholic fiction writer, even during the days, weeks, and hours leading up to her death. She faced her illness and the fact of her mortality with characteristic courage and humor. Reading O'Connor's letters written toward the end of her struggle with the disease that would kill her, one cannot help but hear the voice of a believer, a woman whose faith in God, in the world's goodness (despite evidence to the contrary), and in the promise of eternity was unshakeable. It is the voice of great patience and wondrous love, even in the face of dire affliction. One of the reasons O'Connor could write so knowingly about the Cross is that she knew something of Christ's experience in her own daily life.

Finally, as a fellow Catholic, a fellow laywoman, and a fellow writer, I see in O'Connor an example of a person who has integrated her faith and her art so thoroughly that they have become one practice. In an era wherein such integration is not only rare but is considered by many people in both the secular and sacred realms to be anathema, O'Connor demonstrates that this can be done and done beautifully. Her own art becomes sign and symbol of the creative force that generates and governs the world, and so her writing becomes, both in practice and in fact, a form of sacrament.

When you find something you love, Christ teaches us, you want to give it away. And so I offer this little book as a way to honor Flannery O'Connor's life, art, and faith by making her available to others through better acquaintance with these. In this way, the reader new to O'Connor, as well as the reader familiar with her work, might find Flannery to be a fitting friend, philosopher, and guide along our common journey to the Province of Joy. As writer and mystic Simone Weil once wrote, "Nothing among human things has such power to keep our gaze fixed ever more intensely upon God, than friendship for the friends of God." May this mark the beginning and the deepening of a long and beautiful friendship.

the daily office

Sunday Morning Prayer

GOSPEL MEDITATION

In the sixth month the angel Gabriel was sent by God to a town in Galilee called Nazareth, to a virgin engaged to a man whose name was Joseph, of the house of David. The virgin's name was Mary. And he came to her and said, "Greetings, favored one! The Lord is with you." But she was much perplexed by his words and pondered what sort of greeting this might be. The angel said to her, "Do not be afraid, Mary, for you have found favor with God. And now, you will conceive in your womb and bear a son, and you will name him Jesus. He will be great, and will be called the Son of the Most High, and the Lord God will give to him the throne of his ancestor David. He will reign over the house of Jacob forever, and of his kingdom there will be no end." Mary said to the angel, "How can this be, since I am a virgin?" The angel said to her, "The Holy Spirit will come upon you, and the power of the Most High will overshadow you; therefore the child to be born will be holy; he will be called Son of God. And now, your relative Elizabeth in her old age has also conceived a son; and this is the sixth month for her who was said to be barren. For nothing will be impossible with God." Then Mary said, "Here am I, the servant of the Lord; let it be with me according to your word." Then the angel departed from her. (Luke 1:26–38)

Silence

Invitatory

Lord, open my lips.

> And my mouth will proclaim your praise.

Psalm 100

Make a joyful noise to the Lord, all the earth.

> Worship the Lord with gladness;
> come into his presence with singing.

Know that the Lord is God.

> It is he that made us, and we are his;
> we are his people, the sheep of his pasture.

Enter his gates with thanksgiving,

> and his courts with praise.
> Give thanks to him, bless his name.

For the Lord is good;

> his steadfast love endures forever,
> and his faithfulness to all generations.

Reading

In those days Mary set out and went with haste to a Judean town in the hill country, where she entered the house of Zechariah and greeted Elizabeth. When Elizabeth heard Mary's greeting, the child leaped in her womb. And Elizabeth was filled with the Holy Spirit and exclaimed with a loud cry, "Blessed are you among women, and blessed is the fruit of your womb. And why has this happened to me, that the mother of my Lord comes to me? For as soon as I heard the sound of your greeting, the child in my womb leaped for joy!" (Luke 1:39–44)

LECTIO DIVINA

Either one is serious about salvation or one is not. And it is well to realize that the maximum amount of seriousness admits the maximum amount of comedy. Only if we are secure in our beliefs can we see the comical side of the universe. (MM, 167)

. . .

I went to the Cloisters [Museum] twice and I particularly remember one statue I saw there. . . . It was the Virgin holding the Christ child and both were laughing: not smiling, laughing. I've never seen any models of it anywhere but I was greatly taken with it and should I ever get back to the Cloisters . . . I mean to see if it is there. (HB, 523)

SILENCE

GOSPEL CANTICLE: CANTICLE OF ZECHARIAH
(BENEDICTUS)

Blessed be the Lord, the God of Israel;
He has come to his people and set them free.

He has raised up for us a mighty savior,
born of the house of his servant David.

Through his holy prophets he promised of old
that he would save us from our enemies,
from the hands of all who hate us.

He promised to show mercy to our fathers
and to remember his holy covenant.

This was the oath he swore to our father Abraham:
to set us free from the hands of our enemies,
free to worship without fear,
holy and righteous in his sight all the days of our life.

You, my child, shall be called the prophet of the Most High;
for you will go before the Lord to prepare his way,
to give his people knowledge of salvation
by the forgiveness of their sins.
In the tender compassion of our God,
the dawn from on high shall break upon us,
to shine on those who dwell in darkness
and the shadow of death,
and to guide our feet in the way of peace.

CONCLUSION TO CANTICLE

Glory to the Father, and to the Son, and to the Holy Spirit:
as it was in the beginning, is now, and will be for ever.
Amen. Alleluia.

INTERCESSIONS

Grant me, O Lord, in your infinite goodness, these gifts and graces that I now name:

(Personal Intercessions)

For all these things, I ask in Jesus' name.
Amen.

THE LORD'S PRAYER

Our Father, who art in heaven, hallowed be thy name, thy kingdom come, thy will be done, on earth as it is in heaven. Give us this day our daily bread, and forgive us our trespasses, as we forgive those who trespass against us. And lead us not into temptation, but deliver us from evil.
Amen.

PRAYER OF REFLECTION AND THANKSGIVING

Today, O Lord, I thank you for the gift of joy.

I thank you for the gift of this woman, Mary, who serves as a model of faith and courage, and who teaches the virtue of joy.

The joy she felt in her own body as she conceived this saving Son is an echo of every mother's joy, beginning even with Eve as she conceived her first child and including Sarah as she conceived Isaac.

Her joy is a promise of the greater joys to come as God's divine plan unfolds. It is the joy attested to by Elizabeth, Zechariah, and the infant John, still in his mother's womb, a joy that is fulfilled in the birth of Christ, in his death upon the cross, and in his rising to new life on Easter Morning.

This is a Mystery, Lord, too great for my understanding. Yet I thank you for the continual joy and daily wonder that it brings as I ponder your wonders in my heart. Amen.

PRAYER TO SAINT RAPHAEL

O Raphael, lead us toward those we are waiting for,
> those who are waiting for us:

Raphael, Angel of happy meeting,
> lead us by the hand toward those we are looking for.

May all our movements be guided by your Light
> and transfigured with your joy.

Angel, guide of Tobias,
> lay the request we now address to you at the feet of Him
on whose unveiled Face you are privileged to gaze.
> Lonely and tired, crushed by the separations and sorrows
of life, we feel the need of calling you and of pleading
> for the protection of your wings,
so that we may not be as strangers in the province of joy,
> all ignorant of the concerns of our country.

Remember the weak, you who are strong,
> you whose home lies beyond the region of thunder,
in a land that is always peaceful, always serene and bright
> with the resplendent glory of God.

DISMISSAL

Thank you for the gift of this day, O Lord.
Grant me the grace to go forth to do your will.
Amen.

FURTHER READING AND REFLECTION

In several of her stories, O'Connor mixes tragedy with comedy in profound and sometimes disturbing ways. "A Good Man Is Hard to Find" recounts the story of an escaped convict's encounter with a family on vacation. Though the events of the story are quite grim, and ultimately disastrous, the tale is leavened with details and moments of humor that strike the reader as both troubling and true. O'Connor's rendering of the story reminds us of the paradox of life and of the Christian vision: that comedy will crop up at the most unlikely times and places, just as grace often breaks through during the darkest moments of life. The characters in the story must enact the Way of the Cross (as we are all called to do, in ways both large and small), yet the final fate of the main character—who dies with her legs symbolically crossed and her face smiling up at the heavens—celebrates the salvific nature of the path Christ has walked for (and with) us. O'Connor's paradoxical blend of the tragic and the comic remind us of the paradoxical nature of suffering that leads to joy, of death that leads, finally, to life. This is the essence of the Christian Comedy.

Sunday Evening Prayer

GOSPEL MEDITATION

In the sixth month the angel Gabriel was sent by God to a town in Galilee called Nazareth, to a virgin engaged to a man whose name was Joseph, of the house of David. The virgin's name was Mary. And he came to her and said, "Greetings, favored one! The Lord is with you." But she was much perplexed by his words and pondered what sort of greeting this might be. The angel said to her, "Do not be afraid, Mary, for you have found favor with God. And now, you will conceive in your womb and bear a son, and you will name him Jesus. He will be great, and will be called the Son of the Most High, and the Lord God will give to him the throne of his ancestor David. He will reign over the house of Jacob forever, and of his kingdom there will be no end." Mary said to the angel, "How can this be, since I am a virgin?" The angel said to her, "The Holy Spirit will come upon you, and the power of the Most High will overshadow you; therefore the child to be born will be holy; he will be called Son of God. And now, your relative Elizabeth in her old age has also conceived a son; and this is the sixth month for her who was said to be barren. For nothing will be impossible with God." Then Mary said, "Here am I, the servant of the Lord; let it be with me according to your word." Then the angel departed from her. (Luke 1:26–38)

SILENCE

Opening Prayer

God, come to my assistance.
> Lord, make haste to help me.

Glory to the Father, and to the Son, and to the Holy Spirit:
as it was in the beginning, is now, and will be for ever.
Amen. Alleluia.

Psalm 136:1–9

O give thanks to the Lord, for he is good,
> for his steadfast love endures forever.

O give thanks to the God of gods,
> for his steadfast love endures forever.

O give thanks to the Lord of lords,
> for his steadfast love endures forever;

who alone does great wonders,
> for his steadfast love endures forever;

who by understanding made the heavens,
> for his steadfast love endures forever;

who spread out the earth on the waters,
> for his steadfast love endures forever;

who made the great lights,
> for his steadfast love endures forever;

the sun to rule over the day,
> for his steadfast love endures forever;

the moon and stars to rule over the night,
> for his steadfast love endures forever.

READING

They said to him, "Where is your wife Sarah?" And he said, "There, in the tent." Then one said, "I will surely return to you in due season, and your wife Sarah shall have a son." And Sarah was listening at the tent entrance behind him. Now Abraham and Sarah were old, advanced in age; it had ceased to be with Sarah after the manner of women. So Sarah laughed to herself, saying, "After I have grown old, and my husband is old, shall I have pleasure?" The Lord said to Abraham, "Why did Sarah laugh, and say, 'Shall I indeed bear a child, now that I am old?' Is anything too wonderful for the Lord? At the set time I will return to you, in due season, and Sarah shall have a son." (Genesis 18:9–14)

LECTIO DIVINA

Faith is what you have in the absence of knowledge. The reason this clash doesn't bother me any longer is because I have got, over the years, a sense of the immense sweep of creation, of the evolutionary process in everything, of how incomprehensible God must be to be the God of heaven and earth. You can't fit the Almighty into . . . intellectual categories. (HB, 477)

SILENCE

EXAMINATION OF CONSCIENCE

Assist me, Lord, as I examine the events of this day.
Help me to recognize my sins and omissions and my moments of weakness.

Help me to see those moments of grace and goodness where I
have shown love.

INTERCESSIONS

Grant me, O Lord, in your infinite goodness, these gifts and
graces that I now name:

(Personal Intercessions)

For all these things, I ask in Jesus' name.
Amen.

GOSPEL CANTICLE: MAGNIFICAT

My soul proclaims the greatness of the Lord,
my spirit rejoices in God my Savior
for he has looked with favor on his lowly servant.

From this day all generations will call me blessed:
the Almighty has done great things for me,
and holy is his Name.

He has mercy on those who fear him
in every generation.

He has shown the strength of his arm,
he has scattered the proud in their conceit.

He has cast down the mighty from their thrones,
and has lifted up the lowly.

He has filled the hungry with good things,
and the rich he has sent away empty.

He has come to the help of his servant Israel
for he has remembered his promise of mercy,
the promise he made to our fathers,
to Abraham and his children for ever.

CONCLUSION TO CANTICLE

Glory to the Father, and to the Son, and to the Holy Spirit:
as it was in the beginning, is now, and will be for ever.
Amen. Alleluia.

NUNC DIMITTIS

Lord, now let your servant go in peace;
your word has been fulfilled:

my own eyes have seen the salvation
which you have prepared in the sight of every people:

a light to reveal you to the nations
and the glory of your people Israel.

CONCLUDING PRAYER

May the all-powerful Lord grant me a restful night
and a peaceful death.
Amen.

FURTHER READING AND REFLECTION

Annunciations occur in O'Connor's stories with some regularity, and the "angels" who convey the message take unexpected forms.

In the story "Revelation," Ruby Turpin takes her husband, Claude, to the doctor's office to get treatment for an injury. Claude gets his medication, but more important, Ruby receives a life-saving message from a homely young woman named (appropriately enough) Mary Grace. The message is not a welcome one—it shocks Ruby, follows her home, troubles her sleep. The news about the unhealthy state of her own soul forces her to see herself in a new, unaccustomed light and invites Ruby to change. Ruby is no more prepared for this challenge than Sarah or Mary were. As with these holy women, she is offered a choice: to accept the role God has offered her or to turn away from it. The story depicts the drama of Ruby's wrestling with this angel and the needful message she brings.

Monday Morning Prayer

GOSPEL MEDITATION

For those who want to save their life will lose it, and those who lose their life for my sake will find it. For what will it profit them if they gain the whole world but forfeit their life? (Matthew 16:25–26)

SILENCE

INVITATORY

Lord, open my lips.

And my mouth will proclaim your praise.

PSALM 139:1–18

O Lord, you have searched me and known me.
You know when I sit down and when I rise up;

you discern my thoughts from far away.

You search out my path and my lying down,

and are acquainted with all my ways.

Even before a word is on my tongue,

O Lord, you know it completely.

You hem me in, behind and before,
        and lay your hand upon me.
Such knowledge is too wonderful for me;
        it is so high that I cannot attain it.

Where can I go from your spirit?
        Or where can I flee from your presence?
If I ascend to heaven, you are there;
        if I make my bed in Sheol, you are there.
If I take the wings of the morning
        and settle at the farthest limits of the sea,
even there your hand shall lead me,
        and your right hand shall hold me fast.
If I say, "Surely the darkness shall cover me,
        and the light around me become night,"
even the darkness is not dark to you;
        the night is as bright as the day,
        for darkness is as light to you.

For it was you who formed my inward parts;
        you knit me together in my mother's womb.
I praise you, for I am fearfully and wonderfully made.
        Wonderful are your works;
that I know very well.
        My frame was not hidden from you,
when I was being made in secret,
        intricately woven in the depths of the earth.
Your eyes beheld my unformed substance.
In your book were written
        all the days that were formed for me,
        when none of them as yet existed.

How weighty to me are your thoughts, O God!
>How vast is the sum of them!
I try to count them—they are more than the sand;
>I come to the end—I am still with you.

READING

The next day John again was standing with two of his disciples, and as he watched Jesus walk by, he exclaimed, "Look, here is the Lamb of God!" The two disciples heard him say this, and they followed Jesus. When Jesus turned and saw them following, he said to them, "What are you looking for?" They said to him, "Rabbi" (which translated means Teacher), "where are you staying?" He said to them, "Come and see." They came and saw where he was staying, and they remained with him that day. It was about four o'clock in the afternoon. One of the two who heard John speak and followed him was Andrew, Simon Peter's brother. He first found his brother Simon and said to him, "We have found the Messiah" (which is translated Anointed). He brought Simon to Jesus, who looked at him and said, "You are Simon son of John. You are to be called Cephas" (which is translated Peter). (John 1:35–42)

LECTIO DIVINA

I don't know if anybody can be converted without seeing themselves in a kind of blasting annihilating light, a blast that will last a lifetime. . . . I don't think of conversion as being once and for all and that's that. I think once the process is begun and continues that you are continually turning toward God and away from your own egocentricity and that you have to see this

selfish side of yourself in order to turn away from it. I measure
God by everything that I am not. I begin with that. (HB, 430)

SILENCE

GOSPEL CANTICLE: CANTICLE OF ZECHARIAH
(BENEDICTUS)

Blessed be the Lord, the God of Israel;
He has come to his people and set them free.

He has raised up for us a mighty savior,
born of the house of his servant David.

Through his holy prophets he promised of old
that he would save us from our enemies,
from the hands of all who hate us.

He promised to show mercy to our fathers
and to remember his holy covenant.

This was the oath he swore to our father Abraham:
to set us free from the hands of our enemies,
free to worship without fear,
holy and righteous in his sight all the days of our life.

You, my child, shall be called the prophet of the Most High;
for you will go before the Lord to prepare his way,
to give his people knowledge of salvation
by the forgiveness of their sins.

In the tender compassion of our God,
the dawn from on high shall break upon us,
to shine on those who dwell in darkness
and the shadow of death,
and to guide our feet in the way of peace.

CONCLUSION TO CANTICLE

Glory to the Father, and to the Son, and to the Holy Spirit:
as it was in the beginning, is now, and will be for ever.
Amen. Alleluia.

INTERCESSIONS

Grant me, O Lord, in your infinite goodness, these gifts and
graces that I now name:

(Personal Intercessions)

For all these things, I ask in Jesus' name.
Amen.

THE LORD'S PRAYER

Our Father, who art in heaven, hallowed be thy name, thy
kingdom come, thy will be done, on earth as it is in heaven.
Give us this day our daily bread, and forgive us our trespasses,
as we forgive those who trespass against us. And lead us not
into temptation, but deliver us from evil.
Amen.

Prayer of Reflection and Thanksgiving

Today, O Lord, I thank you for the gift of conversion and its power to make me whom you want me to become.

I thank you for the continual opportunity for rebirth that you offer to me through the examples of your holy ones.

Even St. Paul, who counted himself among the gravest of sinners, was struck from his horse by the force of your love and was taught through blindness to see the need for a radical remaking of himself. So Saul became Paul, through your mercy.

Even St. Peter, not hearing Christ's call, was brought to the Lord by his brother, and Christ claimed him and renamed him. So Simon became Peter, through your grace.

I thank you for changing me, Lord, enabling me to slough off the false self that prevents me from becoming a true follower.

I thank you for your love and compassion that leads me, even when I stray, back to you.
Amen.

Prayer to Saint Raphael

O Raphael, lead us toward those we are waiting for,
> those who are waiting for us:

Raphael, Angel of happy meeting,
> lead us by the hand toward those we are looking for.

May all our movements be guided by your Light
> and transfigured with your joy.

Angel, guide of Tobias,
> lay the request we now address to you at the feet of Him
on whose unveiled Face you are privileged to gaze.
> Lonely and tired, crushed by the separations and sorrows
of life, we feel the need of calling you and of pleading
> for the protection of your wings,
so that we may not be as strangers in the province of joy,
> all ignorant of the concerns of our country.
Remember the weak, you who are strong,
> you whose home lies beyond the region of thunder,
in a land that is always peaceful, always serene and bright
> with the resplendent glory of God.

DISMISSAL

Thank you for the gift of this day, O Lord.
Grant me the grace to go forth to do your will.
Amen.

FURTHER READING AND REFLECTION

Most of the characters in O'Connor's stories are engaged in the process of discovering their true selves. This process is usually preceded by years of static, self-satisfied living, characterized by ignorance, delusion, and denial, and then is set in motion by a violent encounter or shocking discovery.

In "Good Country People," Hulga Hopewell defines herself in terms of her intellectual superiority. Holding a PhD in philosophy, she prides herself on seeing through the pieties and religious delusions of her mother and neighbors, believing she, alone, is in possession of the truth. She has even changed her name from "Joy" to "Hulga," a deliberately ugly name she has made up in order to deny the identity conferred on her by her hopeful mother at her birth. However, Hulga's professed belief in nothing is challenged by a visit from Manley Pointer, a man who claims to be a Bible salesman but proves to be considerably less innocent than he seems. Her encounter with Pointer precipitates an encounter with her true (as opposed to her fabricated) identity. Hulga will never be able to see herself in the same way again.

Monday Evening Prayer

GOSPEL MEDITATION

For those who want to save their life will lose it, and those who lose their life for my sake will find it. For what will it profit them if they gain the whole world but forfeit their life? (Matthew 16:25–26)

SILENCE

OPENING PRAYER

God, come to my assistance.
> Lord, make haste to help me.

Glory to the Father, and to the Son, and to the Holy Spirit: as it was in the beginning, is now, and will be for ever. Amen. Alleluia.

PSALM 131:1–2

O Lord, my heart is not lifted up,
> my eyes are not raised too high;
I do not occupy myself with things
> too great and too marvelous for me.
But I have calmed and quieted my soul,
> like a weaned child with its mother;
> my soul is like the weaned child that is with me.

READING

"Which one of you, having a hundred sheep and losing one of them, does not leave the ninety-nine in the wilderness and go after the one that is lost until he finds it? When he has found it, he lays it on his shoulders and rejoices. And when he comes home, he calls together his friends and neighbors, saying to them, 'Rejoice with me, for I have found my sheep that was lost.' Just so, I tell you, there will be more joy in heaven over one sinner who repents than over ninety-nine righteous persons who need no repentance." (Luke 15:4–7)

LECTIO DIVINA

I am not a mystic and I do not lead a holy life. Not that I can claim any interesting or pleasureable sins (my sense of the devil is strong) but I know all about the garden variety, pride, gluttony, envy and sloth, and what is more to the point, my virtues are as timid as my vices. I think sin occasionally brings one closer to God, but not habitual sin and not this petty kind that blocks every small good. A working knowledge of the devil can be very well had from resisting him. (HB, 92)

SILENCE

EXAMINATION OF CONSCIENCE

Assist me, Lord, as I examine the events of this day.

Help me to recognize my sins and omissions and my moments of weakness.

Help me to see those moments of grace and goodness where I have shown love.

INTERCESSIONS

Grant me, O Lord, in your infinite goodness, these gifts and graces that I now name:

(Personal Intercessions)

For all these things, I ask in Jesus' name.
Amen.

GOSPEL CANTICLE: MAGNIFICAT

My soul proclaims the greatness of the Lord,
my spirit rejoices in God my Savior
for he has looked with favor on his lowly servant.

From this day all generations will call me blessed:
the Almighty has done great things for me,
and holy is his Name.

He has mercy on those who fear him
in every generation.

He has shown the strength of his arm,
he has scattered the proud in their conceit.

He has cast down the mighty from their thrones,
and has lifted up the lowly.

He has filled the hungry with good things,
and the rich he has sent away empty.

He has come to the help of his servant Israel
for he has remembered his promise of mercy,
the promise he made to our fathers,
to Abraham and his children for ever.

Conclusion to Canticle

Glory to the Father, and to the Son, and to the Holy Spirit:
as it was in the beginning, is now, and will be for ever.
Amen. Alleluia.

Nunc Dimittis

Lord, now let your servant go in peace;
your word has been fulfilled:

my own eyes have seen the salvation
which you have prepared in the sight of every people:

a light to reveal you to the nations
and the glory of your people Israel.

Concluding Prayer

May the all-powerful Lord grant me a restful night
and a peaceful death.
Amen.

FURTHER READING AND REFLECTION

The process of self-discovery takes distinct forms in each of O'Connor's stories.

In "Parker's Back," the character of O.E. Parker resists claiming his true identity, even as he is actively engaged in trying to discover who he is. Like Hulga Hopewell in "Good Country People," Parker denies who he is by refusing to claim his own name (Obadiah Elihue) and insisting on being called "O.E." But unlike Hulga, O.E. does not put his faith in the intellect as his source of self-definition. Instead, O.E. looks to the body as a way of knowing his soul: he spends many years acquiring a series of tattoos in the hope of creating a pattern of images on his skin that will reveal to the world (and to himself) the essence of who he is. However, instead of the graceful, articulate pattern he yearns for, his tattoos consist of a series of isolated and meaningless symbols. His perennial dissatisfaction with his tattoos (and the unintegrated self they convey) leads only to more tattoos and, predictably, further dissatisfaction. It takes a violent, near-death experience for Parker to break this pattern and to begin the search in earnest for the self God is calling him to be.

TUESDAY
Blindness & Vision

Tuesday Morning Prayer

GOSPEL MEDITATION

They came to Bethsaida. Some people brought a blind man to
him and begged him to touch him. He took the blind man by
the hand and led him out of the village; and when he had put
saliva on his eyes and laid his hands on him, he asked him, "Can
you see anything?" And the man looked up and said, "I can see
people, but they look like trees, walking." Then Jesus laid his
hands on his eyes again; and he looked intently and his sight
was restored, and he saw everything clearly. (Mark 8:22–25)

SILENCE

INVITATORY

Lord, open my lips.
> And my mouth will proclaim your praise.

PSALM 19:1–8

The heavens are telling the glory of God;
> and the firmament proclaims his handiwork.
Day to day pours forth speech,
> and night to night declares knowledge.

There is no speech, nor are there words;
> their voice is not heard;
yet their voice goes out through all the earth,
> and their words to the end of the world.

In the heavens he has set a tent for the sun,
which comes out like a bridegroom from his wedding canopy,
> and like a strong man runs its course with joy.
Its rising is from the end of the heavens,
> and its circuit to the end of them;
> and nothing is hid from its heat.

The law of the Lord is perfect,
> reviving the soul;
the decrees of the Lord are sure,
> making wise the simple;
the precepts of the Lord are right,
> rejoicing in the heart;
the commandment of the Lord is clear,
> enlightening the eyes.

READING

Now as he was going along and approaching Damascus, suddenly a light from heaven flashed around him. He fell to the ground and heard a voice saying to him, "Saul, Saul, why do you persecute me?" He asked, "Who are you, Lord?" The reply came, "I am Jesus, whom you are persecuting. But get up and enter the city, and you will be told what you are to do." The men who were traveling with him stood speechless because they heard the voice but saw no one. Saul got up from the ground, and though his eyes were open, he could see nothing; so they led him by the hand and brought him into Damascus. For three days he was without sight, and neither ate nor drank.

Now there was a disciple in Damascus named Ananias. The Lord said to him in a vision, "Ananias." He answered, "Here I am, Lord." The Lord said to him, "Get up and go to the street called Straight, and at the house of Judas look for a man of Tarsus named Saul. At this moment he is praying, and he has seen in a vision a man named Ananias come in and lay his hands on him so that he might regain his sight." So Ananias went and entered the house. He laid his hands on Saul and said, "Brother Saul, the Lord Jesus, who appeared to you on your way here, has sent me so that you may regain your sight and be filled with the Holy Spirit." And immediately something like scales fell from his eyes, and his sight was restored. (Acts 9:13–18)

Lectio Divina

[F]aith is a "walking in darkness" and not a theological solution to mystery. The poet is traditionally a blind man, but the Christian poet, and storyteller as well, is like the blind man whom Christ touched, who looked then and saw men as if they were trees, but walking. This is the beginning of vision, and it is an invitation to deeper and stranger visions. (MM, 184–85)

Silence

GOSPEL CANTICLE: CANTICLE OF ZECHARIAH
(BENEDICTUS)

Blessed be the Lord, the God of Israel;
He has come to his people and set them free.

He has raised up for us a mighty savior,
born of the house of his servant David.

Through his holy prophets he promised of old
that he would save us from our enemies,
from the hands of all who hate us.

He promised to show mercy to our fathers
and to remember his holy covenant.

This was the oath he swore to our father Abraham:
to set us free from the hands of our enemies,
free to worship without fear,
holy and righteous in his sight all the days of our life.

You, my child, shall be called the prophet of the Most High;
for you will go before the Lord to prepare his way,
to give his people knowledge of salvation
by the forgiveness of their sins.
In the tender compassion of our God,
the dawn from on high shall break upon us,
to shine on those who dwell in darkness
and the shadow of death,
and to guide our feet in the way of peace.

CONCLUSION TO CANTICLE

Glory to the Father, and to the Son, and to the Holy Spirit:
as it was in the beginning, is now, and will be for ever.
Amen. Alleluia.

INTERCESSIONS

Grant me, O Lord, in your infinite goodness, these gifts and
graces that I now name:

(Personal Intercessions)

For all these things, I ask in Jesus' name.
Amen.

THE LORD'S PRAYER

Our Father, who art in heaven, hallowed be thy name, thy
kingdom come, thy will be done, on earth as it is in heaven.
Give us this day our daily bread, and forgive us our trespasses,
as we forgive those who trespass against us. And lead us not
into temptation, but deliver us from evil.
Amen.

PRAYER OF REFLECTION AND THANKSGIVING

Today, O Lord, I thank you for the gift of vision.

I thank you for the gift of physical vision, which enables me to
enjoy the beauty of the natural world I am able to see and leads
me to ponder the beauty of the supernatural world that I cannot.

I thank you for the gift of spiritual vision, enabling us to see the world as your Son, who is the Light of the World, reveals it to us.

I thank you for the gift of imaginative vision, encouraged and nourished in us by artists and writers, seers who seek, through their work, to reveal the spiritual truth and beauty they perceive.

May I, like the blind man at Bethesda and like St. Paul, be touched by Christ this day and experience both the beginning of vision and the full clarity of sight offered by your word. Amen.

Prayer to Saint Raphael

O Raphael, lead us toward those we are waiting for,
        those who are waiting for us:
Raphael, Angel of happy meeting,
        lead us by the hand toward those we are looking for.
May all our movements be guided by your Light
        and transfigured with your joy.

Angel, guide of Tobias,
        lay the request we now address to you at the feet of Him
on whose unveiled Face you are privileged to gaze.
        Lonely and tired, crushed by the separations and sorrows
of life, we feel the need of calling you and of pleading
        for the protection of your wings,
so that we may not be as strangers in the province of joy,
        all ignorant of the concerns of our country.
Remember the weak, you who are strong,
        you whose home lies beyond the region of thunder,

in a land that is always peaceful, always serene and bright
    with the resplendent glory of God.

DISMISSAL

Thank you for the gift of this day, O Lord.
Grant me the grace to go forth to do your will.
Amen.

FURTHER READING AND REFLECTION

Physical blindness or poor eyesight in O'Connor's stories is
often an indicator of spiritual blindness.

In addition to her self-delusion, the character of Hulga
Hopewell in "Good Country People" is also deluded as to
the true identities of the people around her. She is fooled
spectacularly by the Bible salesman, Manley Pointer, who
proves to be anything but the "good country people" she
believes him to be. At one point in the story, Pointer removes
Hulga's glasses, revealing to both the reader and to herself just
how poor her vision is. Her contempt for the world—and
most everyone in it—is based in her congenital inability to
perceive beauty and goodness. Paradoxically it is only when
her aid to vision is removed that she discovers how blind she
truly is. This is a moment of grace for Hulga and, should she
choose to embrace the new truth she sees, it is, potentially, the
beginning of wisdom.

Tuesday Evening Prayer

Gospel Meditation

They came to Bethsaida. Some people brought a blind man to him and begged him to touch him. He took the blind man by the hand and led him out of the village; and when he had put saliva on his eyes and laid his hands on him, he asked him, "Can you see anything?" And the man looked up and said, "I can see people, but they look like trees, walking." Then Jesus laid his hands on his eyes again; and he looked intently and his sight was restored, and he saw everything clearly. (Mark 8:22–25)

Silence

Opening Prayer

God, come to my assistance.

     Lord, make haste to help me.

Glory to the Father, and to the Son, and to the Holy Spirit:
as it was in the beginning, is now, and will be for ever.
Amen. Alleluia.

Psalm 131:1–2

O Lord, my heart is not lifted up,

     my eyes are not raised too high;

I do not occupy myself with things

     too great and too marvelous for me.

But I have calmed and quieted my soul,

like a weaned child with its mother;
my soul is like the weaned child that is with me.

READING

When I was a child, I spoke like a child, I thought like a child,
I reasoned like a child; when I became an adult, I put an end to
childish ways. For now we see in a mirror, dimly, but then we
will see face to face. (1 Corinthians 13:11–12)

or

Now about eight days after these sayings Jesus took with him
Peter and John and James, and went up on the mountain to pray.
And while he was praying, the appearance of his face changed,
and his clothes became dazzling white. Suddenly they saw two
men, Moses and Elijah, talking to him. They appeared in glory
and were speaking of his departure, which he was about to
accomplish at Jerusalem. Now Peter and his companions were
weighted down with sleep; but since they had stayed awake, they
saw his glory and the two men who stood with him. Just as they
were leaving him, Peter said to Jesus, "Master, it is good for us to
be here; let us make three dwellings, one for you, one for Moses,
and one for Elijah"—not knowing what he said. While he was
saying this, a cloud came and overshadowed them; and they were
terrified as they entered the cloud. Then from the cloud came
a voice that said, "This is my Son, my Chosen; listen to him!"
When the voice had spoken, Jesus was found alone. And they
kept silent and in those days told no one any of the things they
had seen. (Luke 9:28–36)

LECTIO DIVINA

According to St. Thomas, prophetic vision is not a matter of seeing clearly, but of seeing what is distant, hidden. The Church's vision is prophetic vision; it is always widening the view. The ordinary person does not have prophetic vision but he can accept it on faith. St. Thomas also says that prophetic vision is a quality of the imagination, that it does not have anything to do with the moral life of the prophet. It is the imaginative vision itself that endorses the morality. The Church stands for and preserves always what is larger than human understanding. (HB, 365)

SILENCE

EXAMINATION OF CONSCIENCE

Assist me, Lord, as I examine the events of this day.

Help me to recognize my sins and omissions and my moments of weakness.

Help me to see those moments of grace and goodness where I have shown love.

INTERCESSIONS

Grant me, O Lord, in your infinite goodness, these gifts and graces that I now name:

(Personal Intercessions)

For all these things, I ask in Jesus' name.
Amen.

Gospel Canticle: Magnificat

My soul proclaims the greatness of the Lord,
my spirit rejoices in God my Savior
for he has looked with favor on his lowly servant.

From this day all generations will call me blessed:
the Almighty has done great things for me,
and holy is his Name.

He has mercy on those who fear him
in every generation.

He has shown the strength of his arm,
he has scattered the proud in their conceit.

He has cast down the mighty from their thrones,
and has lifted up the lowly.

He has filled the hungry with good things,
and the rich he has sent away empty.

He has come to the help of his servant Israel
for he has remembered his promise of mercy,
the promise he made to our fathers,
to Abraham and his children for ever.

Conclusion to Canticle

Glory to the Father, and to the Son, and to the Holy Spirit:
as it was in the beginning, is now, and will be for ever.
Amen. Alleluia.

Nunc Dimittis

Lord, now let your servant go in peace;
your word has been fulfilled:

my own eyes have seen the salvation
which you have prepared in the sight of every people:

a light to reveal you to the nations
and the glory of your people Israel.

Concluding Prayer

May the all-powerful Lord grant me a restful night
and a peaceful death.
Amen.

Further Reading and Reflection

In O'Connor's novel *Wise Blood*, the character of Hazel Motes is a deeply troubled soul. He feels himself pursued by God and takes desperate measures to evade him. Hazel enacts a willful blindness to God's love and goodness in a number of ways, the most shocking of which is the deliberate blinding of himself. Even the extremity of such an action, however, does not sunder Hazel from the God who searches him and knows him. O'Connor reminds us of the theological fact that just because a soul refuses to see God does not mean God is not there. Paradoxically, it is only after Hazel Motes loses his eyesight that he begins to see.

WEDNESDAY
Limitation & Grace

Wednesday Morning Prayer

GOSPEL MEDITATION

Now there was a woman who had been suffering from hemorrhages for twelve years. She had endured much under many physicians, and had spent all that she had; and she was no better, but rather grew worse. She had heard about Jesus, and came up behind him in the crowd and touched his cloak, for she said, "If I but touch his clothes, I will be made well." Immediately her hemorrhage stopped; and she felt in her body that she was healed of her disease. Immediately aware that power had gone forth from him, Jesus turned about in the crowd and said, "Who touched my clothes?" And his disciples said to him, "You see the crowd pressing in on you; how can you say, 'Who touched me?'" He looked all around to see who had done it. But the woman, knowing what had happened to her, came in fear and trembling, fell down before him, and told him the whole truth. He said to her, "Daughter, your faith has made you well; go in peace, and be healed of your disease." (Mark 5:25–34)

SILENCE

INVITATORY

Lord, open my lips.

> And my mouth will proclaim your praise.

PSALM 42:1–6

As a deer longs for flowing streams,

> so my soul longs for you, O God.

My soul thirsts for God,

> for the living God.

When shall I come and behold

> the face of God?

My tears have been my food

> day and night,

while people say to me continually,

> "Where is your God?"

These things I remember,

> as I pour out my soul:

how I went with the throng,

> and led them in procession to the house of God,

with glad shouts and songs of thanksgiving,

> a multitude keeping festival.

Why are you cast down, O my soul,

> and why are you disquieted within me?

Hope in God; for I shall again praise him,

> my help and my God.

READING

Therefore, since we are justified by faith, we have peace with God through our Lord Jesus Christ, through whom we have obtained access to this grace in which we stand; and we boast in our hope of sharing the glory of God. And not only that, but we also boast in our sufferings, knowing that suffering produces endurance, and endurance produces character, and character produces hope, and hope does not disappoint us, because God's love has been poured into our hearts through the Holy Spirit that has been given to us. (Romans 5:1–5)

LECTIO DIVINA

I have never been anywhere but sick. In a sense, sickness is a place, more instructive than a long trip to Europe, and it's always a place where there's no company; where nobody can follow. Sickness before death is a very appropriate thing and I think those who don't have it miss one of God's mercies. (HB, 163)

SILENCE

GOSPEL CANTICLE: CANTICLE OF ZECHARIAH (BENEDICTUS)

Blessed be the Lord, the God of Israel;
He has come to his people and set them free.

He has raised up for us a mighty savior,
born of the house of his servant David.

Through his holy prophets he promised of old
that he would save us from our enemies,
from the hands of all who hate us.

He promised to show mercy to our fathers
and to remember his holy covenant.

This was the oath he swore to our father Abraham:
to set us free from the hands of our enemies,
free to worship without fear,
holy and righteous in his sight all the days of our life.

You, my child, shall be called the prophet of the Most High;
for you will go before the Lord to prepare his way,
to give his people knowledge of salvation
by the forgiveness of their sins.
In the tender compassion of our God,
the dawn from on high shall break upon us,
to shine on those who dwell in darkness
and the shadow of death,
and to guide our feet in the way of peace.

Conclusion to Canticle

Glory to the Father, and to the Son, and to the Holy Spirit:
as it was in the beginning, is now, and will be for ever.
Amen. Alleluia.

INTERCESSIONS

Grant me, O Lord, in your infinite goodness, these gifts and graces that I now name:

(Personal Intercessions)

For all these things, I ask in Jesus' name.
Amen.

THE LORD'S PRAYER

Our Father, who art in heaven, hallowed be thy name, thy kingdom come, thy will be done, on earth as it is in heaven. Give us this day our daily bread, and forgive us our trespasses, as we forgive those who trespass against us. And lead us not into temptation, but deliver us from evil.
Amen.

PRAYER OF REFLECTION AND THANKSGIVING

Today, O Lord, I thank you for the mystery of affliction that, somehow, brings me closer to you.

Like the psalmist, I, too, resist limitation, unable as I am, with my limited human vision, to see in such suffering the lineaments of grace.

Therefore, I pray for the courage and hope necessary to sustain me, those I know and love, and those I do not know or love, as we endure the challenges and the inevitable pains of mortality that mark us as human.

Enable me to be like the woman in the Gospel whose affliction emboldened her to come close to Christ, to reach out and touch the hem of his garment, and to receive, in return, the healing power of his grace.

Help me Lord, to comprehend this mystery: that the country of sickness and suffering ultimately leads to the Province of Joy. Amen.

PRAYER TO SAINT RAPHAEL

O Raphael, lead us toward those we are waiting for,
      those who are waiting for us:
Raphael, Angel of happy meeting,
      lead us by the hand toward those we are looking for.
May all our movements be guided by your Light
      and transfigured with your joy.

Angel, guide of Tobias,
      lay the request we now address to you at the feet of Him
on whose unveiled Face you are privileged to gaze.
      Lonely and tired, crushed by the separations and sorrows
of life, we feel the need of calling you and of pleading
      for the protection of your wings,
so that we may not be as strangers in the province of joy,
      all ignorant of the concerns of our country.
Remember the weak, you who are strong,
      you whose home lies beyond the region of thunder,
in a land that is always peaceful, always serene and bright
      with the resplendent glory of God.

DISMISSAL

Thank you for the gift of this day, O Lord.
Grant me the grace to go forth to do your will.
Amen.

FURTHER READING AND REFLECTION

O'Connor's stories are full of characters who suffer from physical limitations. Some characters are able to embrace these limitations as a sign of their own humanity and of the humanity of others. Limitation, paradoxically, opens them up, enlarges them, and makes them holy.

In "The Life You Save May Be Your Own," Lucynell Crater's daughter, also named Lucynell, is deaf and mildly retarded. She is also a vision of beauty, even in her affliction, her long, pink-gold hair and innocent gaze indicative of her angelic disposition. Tom T. Shiftlet, who shows up at the Craters' farm one evening, also suffers from a physical limitation. Holding up his arms to greet the women on his arrival, it becomes evident that half of his left arm is missing. However, unlike Lucynell's affliction, Mr. Shiftlet's is indicative of his lack of spiritual wholeness and health. His petulant refusal to acknowledge his imperfection (the birthright of all human beings) is one of many signs of his spiritual pride and blindness. The story dramatizes Mr. Shiftlet's greed and selfishness, his sense of entitlement, as opposed to Lucynell's complete trust and unconditional love. Mr. Shiftlet and Lucynell represent two extremes on the spectrum of possibility when it comes to perceiving the paradox of grace embodied in limitation.

Wednesday Evening Prayer

GOSPEL MEDITATION

Now there was a woman who had been suffering from hemorrhages for twelve years. She had endured much under many physicians, and had spent all that she had; and she was no better, but rather grew worse. She had heard about Jesus, and came up behind him in the crowd and touched his cloak, for she said, "If I but touch his clothes, I will be made well." Immediately her hemorrhage stopped; and she felt in her body that she was healed of her disease. Immediately aware that power had gone forth from him, Jesus turned about in the crowd and said, "Who touched my clothes?" And his disciples said to him, "You see the crowd pressing in on you; how can you say, 'Who touched me?'" He looked all around to see who had done it. But the woman, knowing what had happened to her, came in fear and trembling, fell down before him, and told him the whole truth. He said to her, "Daughter, your faith has made you well; go in peace, and be healed of your disease." (Mark 5:25–34)

SILENCE

OPENING PRAYER

God, come to my assistance.

> Lord, make haste to help me.

Glory to the Father, and to the Son, and to the Holy Spirit: as it was in the beginning, is now, and will be for ever. Amen. Alleluia.

Psalm 51:1–2, 6–7, 10–11

Have mercy on me, O God,
     according to your steadfast love;
according to your abundant mercy
     blot out my transgressions.
Wash me thoroughly from my iniquity,
     and cleanse me from my sin. . . .

You desire truth in the inward being;
     therefore teach me wisdom in my secret heart.
Purge me with hyssop, and I shall be clean;
     wash me, and I shall be whiter than snow. . . .

Create in me a clean heart, O God,
     and put a new and right spirit within me.
Do not cast me away from your presence,
     and do not take your holy spirit from me.

Reading

[T]o keep me from being too elated, a thorn was given me in the flesh, a messenger of Satan to torment me, to keep me from being too elated. Three times I appealed to the Lord about this, that it would leave me, but he said to me, "My grace is sufficient for you, for power is made perfect in weakness." So, I will boast all the more gladly of my weaknesses, so that the power of Christ may dwell in me. Therefore I am content with weaknesses, insults, hardships, persecutions, and calamities for the sake of Christ; for whenever I am weak, then I am strong. (2 Corinthians 12:7–10)

LECTIO DIVINA

All human nature resists grace because grace changes us and the change is painful. . . . Human nature is so faulty that it can resist any amount of grace and most of the time it does. (HB, 307)

or

This notion that grace is healing omits the fact that before it heals, it cuts with the sword Christ said he came to bring. (HB, 411)

SILENCE

EXAMINATION OF CONSCIENCE

Assist me, Lord, as I examine the events of this day.

Help me to recognize my sins and omissions and my moments of weakness.

Help me to see those moments of grace and goodness where I have shown love.

INTERCESSIONS

Grant me, O Lord, in your infinite goodness, these gifts and graces that I now name:

(Personal Intercessions)

For all these things, I ask in Jesus' name.
Amen.

Gospel Canticle: Magnificat

My soul proclaims the greatness of the Lord,
my spirit rejoices in God my Savior
for he has looked with favor on his lowly servant.

From this day all generations will call me blessed:
the Almighty has done great things for me,
and holy is his Name.

He has mercy on those who fear him
in every generation.

He has shown the strength of his arm,
he has scattered the proud in their conceit.

He has cast down the mighty from their thrones,
and has lifted up the lowly.

He has filled the hungry with good things,
and the rich he has sent away empty.

He has come to the help of his servant Israel
for he has remembered his promise of mercy,
the promise he made to our fathers,
to Abraham and his children for ever.

Conclusion to Canticle

Glory to the Father, and to the Son, and to the Holy Spirit:
as it was in the beginning, is now, and will be for ever.
Amen. Alleluia.

Nunc Dimittis

Lord, now let your servant go in peace;
your word has been fulfilled:

my own eyes have seen the salvation
which you have prepared in the sight of every people:

a light to reveal you to the nations
and the glory of your people Israel.

Concluding Prayer

May the all-powerful Lord grant me a restful night
and a peaceful death.
Amen.

Further Reading and Reflection

O'Connor's stories frequently bear out the truth of the beatitudes. Among her favorite themes are Christ's teachings that the last shall be first and that the meek shall inherit the earth. People who are poor and who belong to the lower classes of society, people who suffer from mental and physical illnesses and limitations, and people who suffer from racial and ethnic discrimination figure among the meek in O'Connor's work. They are often despised and held in contempt by (supposedly) more fortunate characters, most of whom also believe themselves to be spiritually, as well as materially, superior to the meek.

In the story "Revelation," Ruby Turpin is one such smug, self-satisfied soul. A series of shocking events in the course of the story, however, lead Ruby to revise her understanding of the role of the meek in God's eschatological plan. In the vision of the heaven heralded by Christ, she comes to understand that those whom she has spent her life domineering and pitying have better seats at the heavenly banquet than she and her equally virtuous husband have. God transforms human afflictions into blessings, and Ruby must learn to live with the paradox that her seeming virtues have relegated her to last place in the procession of saints.

THURSDAY
The Mystery of Incarnation

Thursday Morning Prayer

GOSPEL MEDITATION

In the beginning was the Word, and the Word was with God, and the Word was God. He was in the beginning with God. All things came into being through him, and without him not one thing came into being. What has come into being in him was life, and the life was the light of all people. The light shines in the darkness, and the darkness did not overcome it. (John 1:1–5)

SILENCE

INVITATORY

Lord, open my lips.

     And my mouth will proclaim your praise.

PSALM 139:1–18

O Lord, you have searched me and known me.
You know when I sit down and when I rise up;
     you discern my thoughts from far away.
You search out my path and my lying down,
     and are acquainted with all my ways.

Even before a word is on my tongue,
> O Lord, you know it completely.
You hem me in, behind and before,
> and lay your hand upon me.
Such knowledge is too wonderful for me;
> it is so high that I cannot attain it.

Where can I go from your spirit?
> Or where can I flee from your presence?
If I ascend to heaven, you are there;
> if I make my bed in Sheol, you are there.
If I take the wings of the morning
> and settle at the farthest limits of the sea,
even there your hand shall lead me,
> and your right hand shall hold me fast.
If I say, "Surely the darkness shall cover me,
> and the light around me become night,"
even the darkness is not dark to you;
> the night is as bright as the day,
> for darkness is as light to you.

For it was you who formed my inward parts;
> you knit me together in my mother's womb.
I praise you, for I am fearfully and wonderfully made.
> Wonderful are your works;
that I know very well.
> My frame was not hidden from you,
when I was being made in secret,
> intricately woven in the depths of the earth.
Your eyes beheld my unformed substance.
In your book were written

all the days that were formed for me,
   when none of them as yet existed.
How weighty to me are your thoughts, O God!
   How vast is the sum of them!
I try to count them—they are more than the sand;
   I come to the end—I am still with you.

READING

Jesus said to them, "I am the bread of life. Whoever comes to me will never be hungry, and whoever believes in me will never be thirsty. . . . Very truly, I tell you, unless you eat the flesh of the Son of Man and drink his blood, you have no life in you. Those who eat my flesh and drink my blood have eternal life, and I will raise them up on the last day." . . .

Because of this many of his disciples turned back and no longer went about with him. So Jesus asked the twelve, "Do you also wish to go away?" Simon Peter answered him, "Lord, to whom can we go? You have the words of eternal life." (John 6:35, 53–54, 66–68)

LECTIO DIVINA

[E]very mystery that reaches the human mind, except in the final stages of contemplative prayer, does so by way of the senses. Christ didn't redeem us by a direct intellectual act, but became incarnate in human form, and he speaks to us now through the mediation of a visible Church. All this may seem a long way from the subject of fiction, but it is not, for the main concern of the fiction writer is with mystery as it is incarnated in human life. (MM, 176)

SILENCE

GOSPEL CANTICLE: CANTICLE OF ZECHARIAH
(BENEDICTUS)

Blessed be the Lord, the God of Israel;
He has come to his people and set them free.

He has raised up for us a mighty savior,
born of the house of his servant David.

Through his holy prophets he promised of old
that he would save us from our enemies,
from the hands of all who hate us.

He promised to show mercy to our fathers
and to remember his holy covenant.

This was the oath he swore to our father Abraham:
to set us free from the hands of our enemies,
free to worship without fear,
holy and righteous in his sight all the days of our life.

You, my child, shall be called the prophet of the Most High;
for you will go before the Lord to prepare his way,
to give his people knowledge of salvation
by the forgiveness of their sins.
In the tender compassion of our God,
the dawn from on high shall break upon us,
to shine on those who dwell in darkness

and the shadow of death,
and to guide our feet in the way of peace.

CONCLUSION TO CANTICLE

Glory to the Father, and to the Son, and to the Holy Spirit:
as it was in the beginning, is now, and will be for ever.
Amen. Alleluia.

INTERCESSIONS

Grant me, O Lord, in your infinite goodness, these gifts and
graces that I now name:

(Personal Intercessions)

For all these things, I ask in Jesus' name.
Amen.

THE LORD'S PRAYER

Our Father, who art in heaven, hallowed be thy name, thy
kingdom come, thy will be done, on earth as it is in heaven.
Give us this day our daily bread, and forgive us our trespasses,
as we forgive those who trespass against us. And lead us not
into temptation, but deliver us from evil.
Amen.

PRAYER OF REFLECTION AND THANKSGIVING
Today, O Lord, I thank you for the gift of incarnation.

I thank you for the gift of the creation, which bodies forth your goodness and bounty, and for the gift of my five senses, which enables me to see, hear, taste, touch, and smell the beauty of the universe in its multitudinous forms.

I thank you for the gift of beauty, which inspires in human beings the desire to answer your beauty with creations of our own, making us all artists of the beautiful in imitation of our Maker.

I thank you for the gift of my fellow human beings, each of whom is made in your image and likeness and whose presence, thus, invites me to contemplation of you.

I thank you, Lord, for the central mystery of the Incarnation of God in the world, made manifest to us through the real presence of Christ, both once and forever.

This is a Mystery, Lord, too great for my understanding. Yet I thank you for the continual joy and daily wonder that it brings as I ponder your wonders in my heart.
Amen.

PRAYER TO SAINT RAPHAEL
O Raphael, lead us toward those we are waiting for,
　　　those who are waiting for us:
Raphael, Angel of happy meeting,
　　　lead us by the hand toward those we are looking for.

May all our movements be guided by your Light
  and transfigured with your joy.

Angel, guide of Tobias,
  lay the request we now address to you at the feet of Him
on whose unveiled Face you are privileged to gaze.
  Lonely and tired, crushed by the separations and sorrows
of life, we feel the need of calling you and of pleading
  for the protection of your wings,
so that we may not be as strangers in the province of joy,
  all ignorant of the concerns of our country.
Remember the weak, you who are strong,
  you whose home lies beyond the region of thunder,
in a land that is always peaceful, always serene and bright
  with the resplendent glory of God.

DISMISSAL

Thank you for the gift of this day, O Lord.
Grant me the grace to go forth to do your will.
Amen.

FURTHER READING AND REFLECTION

In her letters and essays, O'Connor explains that the Incarnation figures prominently in her fiction because it is "a unique intervention in history" and is, therefore, "the fulcrum that lifts my particular stories." "It's not a matter in these stories of Do Unto Others. That can be found in any ethical culture series. It is the fact of the Word made flesh" (HB, 227). Indeed, based in her belief that material things of this world serve as vehicles of God's grace, the Word made flesh takes many forms in her stories. No creature, object, or person is too lowly or ordinary to be used by God for his end and purpose, the salvation of the world.

One such person is O.E. Parker of "Parker's Back." Parker becomes obsessed with flesh at the age of fourteen when he sees a brilliantly tattooed man at a fair sideshow. Instead of seeing him as a freak, Parker perceives him to be beautiful, his ordinary flesh transformed into a miraculous vision by the colors and patterns needled into his skin. By contrast, Parker's own poor flesh seems barren and lifeless. Thus begins Parker's quest for the perfect pattern of tattooing that will redeem his own body from the mortal curse of the ordinary. This quest takes Parker places he does not wish to go, yet each choice he makes, however perverse it may seem, brings him closer to his true desire: to perceive the mystery of his own being and the holiness of his poor human flesh. In the course of his journey, Parker is astonished to discover the workings of God in his life at every turn. Unique as his particular journey may be, he is following the ancient pattern of Christian conversion without realizing it.

Thursday Evening Prayer

GOSPEL MEDITATION

In the beginning was the Word, and the Word was with God, and the Word was God. He was in the beginning with God. All things came into being through him, and without him not one thing came into being. What has come into being in him was life, and the life was the light of all people. The light shines in the darkness, and the darkness did not overcome it. (John 1:1–5)

SILENCE

OPENING PRAYER

God, come to my assistance.
>Lord, make haste to help me.

Glory to the Father, and to the Son, and to the Holy Spirit:
as it was in the beginning, is now, and will be for ever.
Amen. Alleluia.

PSALM 25:1–2, 4–5

To you, O Lord, I lift up my soul.
O my God, in you I trust; . . .

Make me to know your ways, O Lord;
>teach me your paths.
Lead me in your truth, and teach me,
>for you are the God of my salvation;
>for you I wait all day long.

READING

O the depth of the riches and wisdom and knowledge of God!
How unsearchable are his judgments and how inscrutable his
ways!

"For who has known the mind of the Lord?
Or who has been his counselor?"
"Or who has given a gift to him,
to receive a gift in return?"

For from him and through him and to him are all things. To
him be the glory forever. Amen. (Romans 11:33–36)

LECTIO DIVINA

What people don't realize is how much religion costs. They
think faith is a big electric blanket, when of course, it is the
cross. . . . Whatever you do anyway, remember that these things
are mysteries and if they were such that we could understand
them, they wouldn't be worth understanding. A God you
understood would be less than yourself. (HB, 354)

SILENCE

EXAMINATION OF CONSCIENCE

Assist me, Lord, as I examine the events of this day.
Help me to recognize my sins and omissions and my moments
of weakness.
Help me to see those moments of grace and goodness where
I have shown love.

INTERCESSIONS

Grant me, O Lord, in your infinite goodness, these gifts and graces that I now name:

(Personal Intercessions)

For all these things, I ask in Jesus' name.
Amen.

GOSPEL CANTICLE: MAGNIFICAT

My soul proclaims the greatness of the Lord,
my spirit rejoices in God my Savior
for he has looked with favor on his lowly servant.

From this day all generations will call me blessed:
the Almighty has done great things for me,
and holy is his Name.

He has mercy on those who fear him
in every generation.

He has shown the strength of his arm,
he has scattered the proud in their conceit.

He has cast down the mighty from their thrones,
and has lifted up the lowly.

He has filled the hungry with good things,
and the rich he has sent away empty.

He has come to the help of his servant Israel
for he has remembered his promise of mercy,
the promise he made to our fathers,
to Abraham and his children for ever.

Conclusion to Canticle

Glory to the Father, and to the Son, and to the Holy Spirit:
as it was in the beginning, is now, and will be for ever.
Amen. Alleluia.

Nunc Dimittis

Lord, now let your servant go in peace;
your word has been fulfilled:

my own eyes have seen the salvation
which you have prepared in the sight of every people:

a light to reveal you to the nations
and the glory of your people Israel.

Concluding Prayer

May the all-powerful Lord grant me a restful night
and a peaceful death.
Amen.

FURTHER READING AND REFLECTION

Mystery is, by definition, that which is hidden or cannot be understood. The characters in O'Connor's stories are constantly grappling with Mystery, and a man or woman's response to the challenge of Mystery is an indicator of the state of his or her soul.

In "A Good Man Is Hard to Find," the criminal nicknamed "the Misfit" refuses to accept the Incarnation and rebels against the supposed holiness of the flesh by perpetrating violence on his fellow human beings. To say that he is a man in spiritual peril is an understatement of huge proportions.

In contrast to this rejection of Mystery, O'Connor gives us Ruby Turpin in "Revelation." Ruby thinks she understands the Incarnation—and this is the beginning of her difficulties. When a series of shocking events challenge her understanding of God and undermine her certainty that she is "saved," Ruby engages in a protracted argument with God. Unable to understand the message he seems to be sending her, she demands an explanation, going even so far as to ask the Maker of the Universe who he thinks he is. God rewards this good (if profoundly flawed) woman in the form of a vision. This epiphany comes to her not in a church, not in a state of prayerful ecstasy, but as she hoses down their so-called Pig Parlor, a concrete yard she and her husband have created for their hogs. (God is, indeed, everywhere, in O'Connor's Incarnational theology.) Mrs. Turpin looks closely at the creatures, all huddled in the corner to escape the violent spraying she has been subjecting them to, and apprehends, for the first time, the mystery of their being, the secret life that animates every living thing in the material world, herself included. She is astonished and profoundly humbled by this revelation. Ruby's openness to Mystery, as opposed to the Misfit's refusal of it, redeems her and sets her on course for a new life in Christ.

FRIDAY
Facing the Dragon

Friday Morning Prayer

GOSPEL MEDITATION

As he was setting out on a journey, a man ran up and knelt before him, and asked him, "Good Teacher, what must I do to inherit eternal life?" Jesus said to him, "Why do you call me good? No one is good but God alone. You know the commandments: 'You shall not murder; You shall not commit adultery; You shall not steal; You shall not bear false witness; You shall not defraud; Honor your father and mother.'" He said to him, "Teacher, I have kept all these since my youth." Jesus, looking at him, loved him and said, "You lack one thing; go, sell what you own, and give the money to the poor, and you will have treasure in heaven; then come, follow me." When he heard this, he was shocked and went away grieving, for he had many possessions. (Mark 10:17–22)

SILENCE

INVITATORY

Lord, open my lips.

> And my mouth will proclaim your praise.

PSALM 23

The Lord is my shepherd, I shall not want.
  He makes me lie down in green pastures;
he leads me beside still waters;
  he restores my soul.
He leads me in right paths
  for his name's sake.

Even though I walk through the darkest valley,
  I fear no evil;
for you are with me;
  your rod and your staff—
  they comfort me.

You prepare a table before me
  in the presence of my enemies;
you anoint my head with oil;
  my cup overflows.
Surely goodness and mercy shall follow me
  all the days of my life,
and I shall dwell in the house of the Lord
  my whole life long.

READING

Jesus said to them again, "Children, how hard it is to enter the kingdom of God! It is easier for a camel to go through the eye of a needle than for someone who is rich to enter the kingdom of God." They were greatly astounded and said to one another, "Then who can be saved?" Jesus looked at them and said, "For mortals it is impossible, but not for God; for all things are possible." (Mark 10:24–27)

Lectio Divina

St. Cyril of Jerusalem, in instructing catechumens, wrote: "The dragon sits by the side of the road, watching those who pass. Beware lest he devour you. We go to the Father of Souls, but it is necessary to pass by the dragon." No matter what form the dragon may take, it is of this mysterious passage past him, or into his jaws, that stories of any depth will always be concerned to tell, and this being the case, it requires considerable courage at any time, in any country, not to turn away from the storyteller. (MM, 35)

Silence

Gospel Canticle: Canticle of Zechariah (Benedictus)

Blessed be the Lord, the God of Israel;
He has come to his people and set them free.

He has raised up for us a mighty savior,
born of the house of his servant David.

Through his holy prophets he promised of old
that he would save us from our enemies,
from the hands of all who hate us.

He promised to show mercy to our fathers
and to remember his holy covenant.

This was the oath he swore to our father Abraham:
to set us free from the hands of our enemies,

free to worship without fear,
holy and righteous in his sight all the days of our life.

You, my child, shall be called the prophet of the Most High;
for you will go before the Lord to prepare his way,
to give his people knowledge of salvation
by the forgiveness of their sins.
In the tender compassion of our God,
the dawn from on high shall break upon us,
to shine on those who dwell in darkness
and the shadow of death,
and to guide our feet in the way of peace.

Conclusion to Canticle

Glory to the Father, and to the Son, and to the Holy Spirit:
as it was in the beginning, is now, and will be for ever.
Amen. Alleluia.

Intercessions

Grant me, O Lord, in your infinite goodness, these gifts and
graces that I now name:

(Personal Intercessions)

For all these things, I ask in Jesus' name.
Amen.

THE LORD'S PRAYER

Our Father, who art in heaven, hallowed be thy name, thy kingdom come, thy will be done, on earth as it is in heaven. Give us this day our daily bread, and forgive us our trespasses, as we forgive those who trespass against us. And lead us not into temptation, but deliver us from evil.
Amen.

PRAYER OF REFLECTION AND THANKSGIVING

Today, O Lord, I thank you for the call to courage that Christ issues to his followers, both in his preaching and by his example.

I thank you for the reminders in Jesus' parables and conversations of the great challenge it is to follow Christ in word and in deed, for I know that the difficulties I experience in trying to be true to my faith are shared by my brothers and sisters, from the first disciples onward.

I thank you, Lord, for the mystery of your mercy, which makes salvation possible, since I am too weak to accomplish it on my own.

I thank you, Lord, for your constant entreaties, "come" and "follow me," even when I have failed to keep your commandments and to live as you would wish me to. For you are, truly, a God of second chances, ever watchful and ever patient as I slowly make my way toward you.

Therefore, in my weakness, I ask your protection and guidance as I continue on my journey, O Father of Souls. May I have the wisdom to recognize spiritual dangers for what they truly are, and may I have the strength to combat them.

I pray this in confidence, as I know that all things are possible with you.
Amen.

Prayer to Saint Raphael

O Raphael, lead us toward those we are waiting for,
       those who are waiting for us:
Raphael, Angel of happy meeting,
       lead us by the hand toward those we are looking for.
May all our movements be guided by your Light
       and transfigured with your joy.

Angel, guide of Tobias,
       lay the request we now address to you at the feet of Him
on whose unveiled Face you are privileged to gaze.
       Lonely and tired, crushed by the separations and sorrows
of life, we feel the need of calling you and of pleading
       for the protection of your wings,
so that we may not be as strangers in the province of joy,
       all ignorant of the concerns of our country.
Remember the weak, you who are strong,
       you whose home lies beyond the region of thunder,
in a land that is always peaceful, always serene and bright
       with the resplendent glory of God.

Dismissal

Thank you for the gift of this day, O Lord.
Grant me the grace to go forth to do your will.
Amen.

Further Reading and Reflection

O'Connor reports her initial discovery of the passage from St. Cyril of Jerusalem quoted above in a letter dated January 1, 1956. Thereafter she returns to the passage again and again because, as her commentary suggests, St. Cyril provides her with a concrete image embodying the truth that lies at the foundation of her fiction: that every good story is about the inevitable confrontation between the individual human person and the force that is most likely to undermine him, body and soul.

"The dragon" takes many forms in O'Connor's stories as each of her protagonists meets a nemesis that challenges everything he or she believes in. The character's response to that shocking and often violent encounter with the enemy determines whether he or she will be destroyed or will be able to continue along the road to salvation.

Nowhere is this pattern more evident than in the conflict between the Misfit and the Grandmother in "A Good Man Is Hard to Find." In fact, the passage served as epigraph to the collection in which "A Good Man" served as the title story. The Grandmother, who has lived her long life assuming herself to be a good and faithful Christian, finds that faith and goodness tested sorely by the Misfit, who refuses to believe in Christ and the possibility of redemption. The two engage in increasingly desperate theological argument, even as his henchmen systematically carry out the murder of her family. In the end, the Grandmother, confronted with the inevitability of her own death, must choose how to respond to this onslaught of evil that has befallen her. The choice she makes surprises everyone, herself included, and the Misfit most of all. In her moment of truth, even she—a garrulous, foolish, flawed old woman—is able to best the dragon, dreadful as he proves to be, thereby giving hope to us all.

———————❦———————

Friday Evening Prayer

GOSPEL MEDITATION

Now Peter was sitting outside in the courtyard. A servant-girl came to him and said, "You were with Jesus the Galilean." But he denied it before all of them, saying, "I do not know what you are talking about." When he went out to the porch, another servant-girl saw him, and she said to the bystanders, "This man was with Jesus of Nazareth." Again he denied it with an oath, "I do not know the man." After a little while the bystanders came up and said to Peter, "Certainly you are also one of them, for your accent betrays you." Then he began to curse, and he swore an oath, "I do not know the man!" At that moment the cock crowed. Then Peter remembered what Jesus had said: "Before the cock crows, you will deny me three times." And he went out and wept bitterly. (Matthew 26:69–75)

SILENCE

OPENING PRAYER

God, come to my assistance.

Lord, make haste to help me.

Glory to the Father, and to the Son, and to the Holy Spirit: as it was in the beginning, is now, and will be for ever. Amen. Alleluia.

PSALM 51:1-2, 6-7, 10-11

Have mercy on me, O God,
  according to your steadfast love;
according to your abundant mercy
  blot out my transgressions.
Wash me thoroughly from my iniquity,
  and cleanse me from my sin. . . .

You desire truth in the inward being,
  therefore teach me wisdom in my secret heart.
Purge me with hyssop, and I shall be clean,
  wash me, and I shall be whiter than snow. . . .

Create in me a clean heart, O God,
  and put a new and right spirit within me.
Do not cast me away from your presence,
  and do not take your holy spirit from me.

READING

"Enter through the narrow gate; for the gate is wide and the road is easy that leads to destruction, and there are many who take it. For the gate is narrow and the road hard that leads to life, and there are few who find it." (Matthew 7:13–14)

LECTIO DIVINA
(Repeated from the Morning)

St. Cyril of Jerusalem, in instructing catechumens, wrote: "The dragon sits by the side of the road, watching those who pass. Beware lest he devour you. We go to the Father of Souls, but it is necessary to pass by the dragon." No matter what form the dragon may take, it is of this mysterious passage past him, or into his jaws, that stories of any depth will always be concerned to tell, and this being the case, it requires considerable courage at any time, in any country, not to turn away from the storyteller. (MM, 35)

SILENCE

EXAMINATION OF CONSCIENCE

Assist me, Lord, as I examine the events of this day.

Help me to recognize my sins and omissions and my moments of weakness.

Help me to see those moments of grace and goodness where I have shown love.

INTERCESSIONS

Grant me, O Lord, in your infinite goodness, these gifts and graces that I now name:

(Personal Intercessions)

For all these things, I ask in Jesus' name.
Amen.

Gospel Canticle: Magnificat

My soul proclaims the greatness of the Lord,
my spirit rejoices in God my Savior
for he has looked with favor on his lowly servant.

From this day all generations will call me blessed:
the Almighty has done great things for me,
and holy is his Name.

He has mercy on those who fear him
in every generation.

He has shown the strength of his arm,
he has scattered the proud in their conceit.

He has cast down the mighty from their thrones,
and has lifted up the lowly.

He has filled the hungry with good things,
and the rich he has sent away empty.

He has come to the help of his servant Israel
for he has remembered his promise of mercy,
the promise he made to our fathers,
to Abraham and his children for ever.

Conclusion to Canticle

Glory to the Father, and to the Son, and to the Holy Spirit:
as it was in the beginning, is now, and will be for ever.
Amen. Alleluia.

Nunc Dimittis

Lord, now let your servant go in peace;
your word has been fulfilled:

my own eyes have seen the salvation
which you have prepared in the sight of every people:

a light to reveal you to the nations
and the glory of your people Israel.

Concluding Prayer

May the all-powerful Lord grant me a restful night
and a peaceful death.
Amen.

Further Reading and Reflection

St. Cyril's image of the dragon serves as *lectio divina* for both
morning and evening prayer on Friday, the day Christians
commemorate the crucifixion, reminding us of Christ's vic-
tory over the Dragon, and of the inevitability of our own
encounter. In the case of O'Connor's characters, suffering nearly always occurs as a result of the meeting with the
Dragon. However, the image of the crucified Christ reminds
us of the fact that such suffering can be redemptive and,
therefore, healing.

The character of Julian in "Everything That Rises Must
Converge" endures what he believes to be excruciating
agony in having to live with his mother and put up with her
foolish attachment to the supposedly "good old days" of the

South's former glory. Like many people of her generation, she maintains hopelessly mistaken ideas about race, and Julian looks forward to the day he can prove her racism wrong and break her spirit. Inevitably, that day arrives, and Julian greets it with glee. Riding on the bus one evening, he and his mother encounter a large African American woman who is wearing a hat identical to the one worn by his mother. Julian goads his mother, attempting to humble her by insisting upon equality between the two women symbolized by the identical hats. The African American woman seems to him a God-send, a means though which he can teach his mother a sorely needed lesson. However, the lesson goes terribly wrong when his mother makes a well-intended gesture toward the woman's son and receives, in return, a violent blow, one which, ultimately, kills her. In the final moments of the story, Julian discovers that the encounter he so fervently desired has destroyed the person he loves most in the world. He makes the acquaintance of genuine, rather than imagined, suffering, and the reader is left to wonder whether the encounter will destroy him as well, or whether it might prove to be a source of saving grace.

Saturday Morning Prayer

GOSPEL MEDITATION
"I believe. Help my unbelief!" (Mark 9:24)

SILENCE

INVITATORY
Lord, open my lips.
>   And my mouth will proclaim your praise.

PSALM 27:1–3, 5, 7–9, 13–14
The Lord is my light and my salvation;
>   whom should I fear?
The Lord is the stronghold of my life;
>   of whom should I be afraid?

When evildoers assail me
>   to devour my flesh—
my adversaries and foes—
>   they shall stumble and fall.

Though an army encamp against me,
>   my heart shall not fear;

though war rise up against me,
> yet I will be confident. . . .

For he will hide me in his shelter
> in the day of trouble;
he will conceal me under the cover of his tent;
> he will set me high on a rock. . . .

Hear, O Lord, when I cry aloud,
> be gracious to me and answer me!
"Come," my heart says, "seek his face!"
> Your face, Lord, do I seek.
> Do not hide your face from me.

Do not turn your servant away in anger,
> you who have been my help.
Do not case me off, do not forsake me,
> O God of my salvation! . . .

I believe that I shall see the goodness of the Lord
> in the land of the living.
Wait for the Lord;
> be strong, and let your heart take courage;
> wait for the Lord!

READING

Peter answered him, "Lord, if it is you, command me to come to you on the water." He said, "Come." So Peter got out of the boat, started walking on the water, and came toward Jesus. But when he noticed the strong wind, he became frightened, and beginning to sink, he cried out, "Lord, save me!" Jesus immediately reached out his hand and caught him, saying to him, "You of little faith, why did you doubt?" When they go into the boat, the wind ceased. And those in the boat worshiped him, saying, "Truly you are the Son of God." (Matthew 14: 28–33)

LECTIO DIVINA

When I ask myself how I know I believe, I have no satisfactory answer at all, no assurance at all, no feeling at all. I can only say with Peter, Lord I believe, help my unbelief. All I can say about my love of God, is, Lord help me in my lack of it. (HB, 92)

SILENCE

GOSPEL CANTICLE: CANTICLE OF ZECHARIAH (BENEDICTUS)

Blessed be the Lord, the God of Israel;
He has come to his people and set them free.

He has raised up for us a mighty savior,
born of the house of his servant David.

Through his holy prophets he promised of old
that he would save us from our enemies,
from the hands of all who hate us.

He promised to show mercy to our fathers
and to remember his holy covenant.

This was the oath he swore to our father Abraham:
to set us free from the hands of our enemies,
free to worship without fear,
holy and righteous in his sight all the days of our life.

You, my child, shall be called the prophet of the Most High;
for you will go before the Lord to prepare his way,
to give his people knowledge of salvation
by the forgiveness of their sins.
In the tender compassion of our God,
the dawn from on high shall break upon us,
to shine on those who dwell in darkness
and the shadow of death,
and to guide our feet in the way of peace.

CONCLUSION TO CANTICLE

Glory to the Father, and to the Son, and to the Holy Spirit:
as it was in the beginning, is now, and will be for ever.
Amen. Alleluia.

INTERCESSIONS

Grant me, O Lord, in your infinite goodness, these gifts and
graces that I now name:

(Personal Intercessions)

For all these things, I ask in Jesus' name.
Amen.

The Lord's Prayer

Our Father, who art in heaven, hallowed be thy name, thy kingdom come, thy will be done, on earth as it is in heaven. Give us this day our daily bread, and forgive us our trespasses, as we forgive those who trespass against us. And lead us not into temptation, but deliver us from evil.

Amen.

Prayer of Reflection and Thanksgiving

Today, O Lord, I thank you for the gift of belief.

I thank you for the examples of your disciples, courageous in their attempts to remain faithful to you even when their (merely) human resolve faltered.

I thank you, Lord, for the mystery of faith that enables me to believe where I cannot prove, to embrace intuition rather than demanding evidence, to feel your saving presence even when I am walking in darkness.

I thank you, Lord, for your constant invitations to me to walk with you on water, even though, like Peter, I am slow to accept and sometimes blind to the grace that buoys me up in the midst of the storm.

I thank you, Lord, for those revelations of your immanence in the world, both seen and unseen, and for the resurrections within my own soul at these recoveries and rediscoveries of you.

I ask you for your continued patience with me, Lord, even as I am assailed by my own bouts of doubt, fear, and near despair.

Lord, I believe. Help me in my unbelief.
Amen.

Prayer to Saint Raphael

O Raphael, lead us toward those we are waiting for,
        those who are waiting for us:
Raphael, Angel of happy meeting,
        lead us by the hand toward those we are looking for.
May all our movements be guided by your Light
        and transfigured with your joy.

Angel, guide of Tobias,
        lay the request we now address to you at the feet of Him
on whose unveiled Face you are privileged to gaze.
        Lonely and tired, crushed by the separations and sorrows
of life, we feel the need of calling you and of pleading
        for the protection of your wings,
so that we may not be as strangers in the province of joy,
        all ignorant of the concerns of our country.
Remember the weak, you who are strong,
        you whose home lies beyond the region of thunder,
in a land that is always peaceful, always serene and bright
        with the resplendent glory of God.

Dismissal

Thank you for the gift of this day, O Lord.
Grant me the grace to go forth to do your will.
Amen.

FURTHER READING AND REFLECTION

Scripture and saint's lives are full of stories of men and women who suffer, from time to time, the affliction of doubt. Faith comes and goes, like the tide, and often deserts even the holiest of men and women at those moments when they need it most. O'Connor's characters suffer from bouts of doubt as well, usually brought on by moments of extremity. In "A Good Man Is Hard to Find," the Grandmother finds herself questioning the basic tenets of her long belief in Christianity as a result of her encounter with the Misfit. This is, most likely, the Grandmother's first genuine engagement with atheism. After a lifetime of being surrounded by people who have professed belief in Christianity (a belief largely untried and untested), she finds herself face-to-face with a truly dangerous man—one who believes in nothing—and doesn't know how to respond. As he calmly goes about the business of murdering her family, she struggles to present moral arguments against his behavior, as this is the final, and only, defense left to her. The Misfit, however, is steadfast in his unbelief, so much so that the Grandmother begins to doubt her own faith. At her lowest moment, she confesses this confusion, provoking in the Misfit a confession of his own agony of doubt. This is the point at which the story turns, for the Grandmother's profound belief, which she seemed unable to express with words, becomes evident in her actions. It is, in fact, a gesture of love that gets her killed, in the end; however, this final act of charity saves her, as is evident from her willingness to risk death for the sake of another, undeserving of her love as he may be. Even the Misfit recognizes her sacrifice, and the conclusion of the story holds out the hope (however slight) that her action may serve as a seed planted in the soil of his own barren soul and that faith may, one day, blossom there as it did in the doubting Grandmother's soul.

Saturday Evening Prayer

GOSPEL MEDITATION
"I believe. Help my unbelief!" (Mark 9:24)

SILENCE

OPENING PRAYER

God, come to my assistance.

  Lord, make haste to help me.

Glory to the Father, and to the Son, and to the Holy Spirit:
as it was in the beginning, is now, and will be for ever.
Amen. Alleluia.

PSALM 40:1–3

I waited patiently for the Lord;

  he inclined to me and heard my cry.

He drew me up from the desolate pit,

  out of the miry bog,

and set my feet upon a rock,

  making my steps secure.

He put a new song in my mouth,

  a song of praise to our God.

READING

Mary stood weeping outside the tomb. As she wept, she bent over to look into the tomb; and she saw two angels in white, sitting where the body of Jesus had been lying, one at the head and the other at the feet. They said to her, "Woman, why are you weeping?" She said to them, "They have taken away my Lord, and I do not know where they have laid him." When she had said this, she turned around and saw Jesus standing there, but she not know that it was Jesus. Jesus said to her, "Woman, why are you weeping? Whom are you looking for?" Supposing him to be the gardener, she said to him, "Sir, if you have carried him away, tell me where you have laid him, and I will take him away." Jesus said to her, "Mary!" She turned and said to him, in Hebrew, "Rabbouni!" (John 20:11–16)

LECTIO DIVINA

I think that this experience you are having of losing your faith, or as you think, of having lost it, is an experience that in the long run belongs to faith. . . . I don't know how the kind of faith required of a Christian . . . can be at all if it is not grounded on this experience . . . of unbelief. . . . Peter said, "Lord, I believe. Help my unbelief." It is the most natural and most human and most agonizing prayer in the gospels, and I think it is the foundation prayer of faith. (HB, 476)

SILENCE

Examination of Conscience

Assist me, Lord, as I examine the events of this day.

Help me to recognize my sins and omissions and my moments of weakness.

Help me to see those moments of grace and goodness where I have shown love.

Intercessions

Grant me, O Lord, in your infinite goodness, these gifts and graces that I now name:

(Personal Intercessions)

For all these things, I ask in Jesus' name.
Amen.

Gospel Canticle: Magnificat

My soul proclaims the greatness of the Lord,
my spirit rejoices in God my Savior
for he has looked with favor on his lowly servant.

From this day all generations will call me blessed:
the Almighty has done great things for me,
and holy is his Name.

He has mercy on those who fear him
in every generation.

He has shown the strength of his arm,
he has scattered the proud in their conceit.

He has cast down the mighty from their thrones,
and has lifted up the lowly.

He has filled the hungry with good things,
and the rich he has sent away empty.

He has come to the help of his servant Israel
for he has remembered his promise of mercy,
the promise he made to our fathers,
to Abraham and his children for ever.

Conclusion to Canticle

Glory to the Father, and to the Son, and to the Holy Spirit:
as it was in the beginning, is now, and will be for ever.
Amen. Alleluia.

Nunc Dimittis

Lord, now let your servant go in peace;
your word has been fulfilled:

my own eyes have seen the salvation
which you have prepared in the sight of every people:

a light to reveal you to the nations
and the glory of your people Israel.

CONCLUDING PRAYER

May the all-powerful Lord grant me a restful night
and a peaceful death.
Amen.

FURTHER READING AND REFLECTION

In "Revelation," Ruby Turpin's world is rocked when she is struck in the eye with a book thrown by a young woman who sees, despises, and publicly denounces Ruby's spiritual complacency and pride. All of her life Ruby has believed herself to be a good, generous soul, blessed and beloved by God, until this young woman tells her, in no uncertain terms, that her true home is hell rather than heaven. Ruby's understanding of the universe immediately begins to unravel and she returns home to wrestle with the seemingly impossible paradox of herself as half-sinner, half-saint and of a God who both loves her and loathes her flaws.

To her credit, Ruby never doubts the existence of God, but she does doubt his wisdom and power, calling both into question in the course of an impassioned harangue, in which she urges the God of the universe to justify his ineffable ways to her. Ruby receives an explanation in the form of a vision that enables her to see the road to salvation as Christ actually described it rather than as she mistakenly imagined it. The god Ruby worshiped previously was an idol of her own making, one who looked, coincidentally, very much like herself in the same way that his supposed "justice" resembled her own.

By the conclusion of the story, the image of that false god is dead, supplanted by this vision of the true God. In much the same way, the old Ruby Turpin has died to her old life and been reborn to a new one. She finally understands that her contempt for her fellow human beings and self-congratulation have no place in the kingdom of heaven, overseen by a God of infinite and unconditional love. Her conversion is nothing less than a resurrection, a foretaste of the final one that will bring her and all the dead to eternal life in Christ.

occasions for meditation

FAVORED PRAYERS, POEMS & PROSE PASSAGES

A Gathering of Devotional Poems

Gerard Manley Hopkins

PIED BEAUTY

Glory be to God for dappled things—
 For skies of couple-colour as a brinded cow;
  For rose-moles all in stipple upon trout that swim;
Fresh-firecoal chestnut-falls; finches' wings;
 Landscape plotted and pieced—fold, fallow, and plough;
  And áll trades, their gear and tackle and trim.
All things counter, original, spáre, strange;
 Whatever is fickle, frecklèd (who knows how?)
  With swíft, slów; sweet, sóur; adázzle, dím;
He fathers-forth whose beauty is pást change:

   Práise hím.

GOD'S GRANDEUR

The world is charged with the grandeur of God.
    It will flame out, like shining from shook foil;
    It gathers to a greatness, like the ooze of oil
Crushed. Why do men then now not reck his rod?
Generations have trod, have trod, have trod;
    And all is seared with trade; bleared, smeared with toil;
    And wears man's smudge and shares man's smell: the soil
Is bare now, nor can foot feel, being shod.

And for all this, nature is never spent;
    There lives the dearest freshness deep down things;
And though the last lights off the black West went
    Oh, morning, at the brown brink eastward, springs—
Because the Holy Ghost over the bent
    World broods with warm breast and with ah! bright wings.

SPRING AND FALL

to a Young Child

Margaret, are you grieving
Over Goldengrove unleaving?
Leaves, like the things of man, you
With your fresh thoughts care for, can you?
Ah! as the heart grows older
It will come to such sights colder
By and by, nor spare a sigh

Though worlds of wanwood leafmeal lie;
And yet you *will* weep and know why.
Now no matter, child, the name:
Sorrow's springs are the same.
Nor mouth had, no nor mind, expressed
What héart héard of, ghóst guéssed:
It is the blight man was born for,
It is Margaret you mourn for.

Thou Art Indeed Just, Lord

*Justus quidem tu es, Domine, si disputem tecum; verumtamen justa
loquar ad te: Quare via impiorum prosperatur? &c.*

Thou art indeed just, Lord, if I contend
With thee; but, sir, so what I plead is just.
Why do sinners' ways prosper? and why must
Disappointment all I endeavor end?

   Wert thou my enemy, O thou my friend,
How wouldst thou worse, I wonder, than thou dost
Defeat, thwart me? Oh, the sots and thralls of lust
Do in spare hours more thrive than I that spend,
Sir, life upon thy cause. See, banks and brakes
Now leavèd how thick! lacèd they are again
With fretty chervil, look, and fresh wind shakes
Them; birds build—but not I build; no, but strain,
Time's eunuch, and not breed one work that wakes.
Mine, O thou lord of life, send my roots rain.

John Donne

A HYMN TO GOD THE FATHER

I.
Wilt Thou forgive that sin where I begun,
            Which was my sin, though it were done before?
Wilt Thou forgive that sin, through which I run,
            And do run still, though still I do deplore?
When Thou hast done, Thou hast not done,
            For I have more.

II.
Wilt Thou forgive that sin which I have won
            Others to sin, and made my sin their door?
Wilt Thou forgive that sin which I did shun
            A year or two, but wallowed in a score?
When Thou hast done, Thou hast not done,
            For I have more.

III.
I have a sin of fear, that when I have spun
            My last thread, I shall perish on the shore;
But swear by Thyself, that at my death Thy Son
            Shall shine as He shines now, and heretofore;
And having done that, Thou hast done;
            I fear no more.

DEATH BE NOT PROUD

Death be not proud, though some have called thee
Mighty and dreadful, for, thou art not so,
For, those, whom thou think'st, thou dost overthrow,
Die not, poor death, nor yet canst thou kill me.
From rest and sleep, which but thy pictures be,
Much pleasure, then from thee, much more must flow,
And soonest our best men with thee do go,
Rest of their bones, and soul's delivery.
Thou art slave to Fate, Chance, kings, and desperate men,
And dost with poison, war, and sickness dwell,
And poppy, or charms can make us sleep as well,
And better then thy stroke; why swell'st thou then?
One short sleep past, we wake eternally,
And death shall be no more; death, thou shalt die.

HYMN TO GOD, MY GOD, IN MY SICKNESS

Since I am coming to that holy room,
     Where, with thy choir of saints for evermore,
I shall be made thy music; as I come
     I tune the instrument here at the door,
     And what I must do then, think here before.

Whilst my physicians by their love are grown
     Cosmographers, and I their map, who lie
Flat on this bed, that by them may be shown
     That this is my south-west discovery,
     Per fretum febris, by these straits to die,

I joy, that in these straits I see my west;
      For, though their currents yield return to none,
What shall my west hurt me? As west and east
      In all flat maps (and I am one) are one,
      So death doth touch the resurrection.

Is the Pacific Sea my home? Or are
      The eastern riches? Is Jerusalem?
Anyan, and Magellan, and Gibraltar,
      All straits, and none but straits, are ways to them,
      Whether where Japhet dwelt, or Cham, or Shem.

We think that Paradise and Calvary,
      Christ's cross, and Adam's tree, stood in one place;
Look, Lord, and find both Adams met in me;
      As the first Adam's sweat surrounds my face,
      May the last Adam's blood my soul embrace.

So, in his purple wrapp'd, receive me, Lord;
      By these his thorns, give me his other crown;
And as to others' souls I preach'd thy word,
      Be this my text, my sermon to mine own:
      "Therefore that he may raise, the Lord throws down."

Blessed John Henry Newman

LEAD, KINDLY LIGHT

Lead, kindly Light, amid the encircling gloom,
Lead thou me on!
The night is dark, and I am far from home,
Lead thou me on!
Keep thou my feet; I do not ask to see
The distant scene, one step enough for me.

I was not ever thus, nor prayed that thou
Shouldst lead me on:
I loved to choose and see my path, but now
Lead thou me on!
I loved the garish days, and, spite of fears,
Pride ruled my will: remember not past years.

So long thy power hath blessed me, sure it still
Will lead me on;
O'er moor and fen, o'er crag and torrent, till
The night is gone;
And with the morn those angel faces smile
Which I have loved long since, and lost awhile.

Prayers and Sayings of the Saints

Do you not know, my friend, that you owe the first fruits of your heart and voice to God?

—St. Ambrose *on Psalm 118*

Late have I loved you, beauty so old and so new, late have I loved you! And indeed you were within and I was without, and there I sought you and rushed, unbeautiful, after those beautiful things you have made. You were with me and I was not with you. Things held me far from you: things which, if they were not in you, would not be at all. You called and shouted and penetrated my deafness. You flashed and shone and put my blindness to flight. You wafted your perfume and I breathed in and I pant for you. I tasted and I hunger and thirst. You touched me and I went on fire for your peace.

—St. Augustine of Hippo

You have made us for yourself and our heart is restless until it rests in you.

—St. Augustine of Hippo

Grant me, O Lord my God,
a mind to know you,
a heart to seek you,
wisdom to find you,
conduct pleasing to you,

faithful perseverance in waiting for you,
and a hope of finally embracing you.

—St. Thomas Aquinas

Deeply I adore you, veiled divinity
underneath the signs I see you are truly here
and to you I surrender, Love so strong so near
contemplating you, my Love, leads to ecstasy.

Now I turn to you in faith: you are veiled from me
hidden Jesus, hear my prayer, grant this longed-for grace
bring me out of the shadowlands, let me see your face
in your glory let me find joy eternally. Amen.

—St. Thomas Aquinas

Eternal Trinity: you are the Creator and I am the creature. And you have enlightened me to know that in your re-making of me through the blood of your only-begotten Son you fell in love with the beauty of what you had made. . . . In the mirror of this light I know you the supreme good, the good beyond all good . . . the beauty beyond all beauty, the wisdom beyond all wisdom. . . . You feast us who are famished on your sweetness because you are sweet without any bitterness, eternal Trinity!

—St. Catherine of Siena

Let nothing upset you,
Let nothing frighten you.
Everything is changing.

God alone is changeless.
Patience attains the goal.
Who has God lacks nothing.
God alone fills all her needs.

—St. Teresa of Avila

The important thing is not to think much, but to love much; and so do that which best stirs you to love.

—St. Teresa of Avila

Pregnant with the holy
Word will come the Virgin
walking down the road
if you will take her in.

—St. John of the Cross

Here am I, the servant of the Lord; let it be with me according to your word.

—Mary, Mother of Jesus *(Luke 1:38)*

Take, Lord, and receive all my liberty, my memory, my understanding, and all my will, all that I have and possess. You have given it to me: to you, Lord, I return it; all is yours: dispose of it entirely as you will. Give me your love and grace, for that is enough for me.

—St. Ignatius of Loyola

On Grace, Mystery & Mortality:
Prose Passages

Do not be always wanting everything to turn out as you think it should, but rather as God pleases, then you will be undisturbed and thankful in your prayer.

—ABBA NILUS, *The Sayings of the Desert Fathers*

Love in action is a harsh and dreadful thing compared with love in dreams.

—FYODOR DOSTOYEVSKY, *The Brothers Karamazov*

Throughout my whole life, during every moment I have lived, the world has gradually been taking on light and fire for me, until it has come to envelope me in one mass of luminosity, glowing from within. . . . The purple flush of matter fading imperceptibly into the gold of spirit, to be lost finally in the incandescence of a personal universe.

—TEILHARD DE CHARDIN, *The Divine Milieu*

Abbot Lot came to Abbot Joseph and said: "Father, according to my strength, I keep a moderate rule of prayer and fasting, quiet and meditation, and as far as I can, I control my imagination; what more must I do?" And the old man rose and held his hands to the sky so that his fingers became like flames of fire, and he said "If you will, you shall become all flame."

—ABBA JOSEPH OF PANEPHYSIS, *The Sayings of the Desert Fathers*

Love all God's creation, the whole and every grain of sand of it. Love every leaf, every ray of God's light. Love the animals, love the plants, love everything. If you love everything, you will perceive the divine mystery in things. Once you perceive it, you will begin to comprehend it better every day. And you will come at last to love the whole world with an all-embracing love.

—FYODOR DOSTOYEVSKY, *The Brothers Karamazov*

By virtue of the Creation and, still more of the Incarnation, *nothing* here below is *profane* for those who know how to see.

—TEILHARD DE CHARDIN, *The Divine Milieu*

Sometimes by secret stirrings, sometimes by the promptings of circumstance, God recalls the soul to itself. In the most unexpected ways he makes it aware of its wretchedness. . . . His hand is ever present to recreate and restore what he has made. Furthermore, he knows how to make use of the evil that man does, for he does not cease to bring into order what he condemns; though he does not create it, yet he orders it to the good.

—JEAN GUITTON, *The Modernity of St. Augustine*

History reveals God's method to us. Suffering is an element of it. But suffering in itself does not purify. It has too often and unthinkingly been said that it does. No, suffering and failure are an intervention of God meant to prevent man from *settling* in a condition that is not his vocation, which is beatitude.

—CLAUDE TRESMONTANT, *A Study of Hebrew Thought*

Like an artist who is able to make use of a fault or an impurity in the stone he is sculpting or the bronze he is casting so as to produce more exquisite lines or a more beautiful tone, God, without sparing us the partial deaths, nor the final death, which form an essential part of our lives, transfigures them by integrating them in a better plan—provided we lovingly trust in him. Not only our unavoidable ills but our faults, even our most deliberate ones, can be embraced in that transformation, *provided always we repent of them.* Not everything is immediately good to those who seek God; but everything is capable of becoming good: *omnia convertuntur in bonum.*

—Teilhard de Chardin, *The Divine Milieu*

All religious reality begins with what Biblical religion calls the "fear of God." It comes when our existence between birth and death becomes incomprehensible and uncanny, when all security is shattered through mystery, the inscrutableness of which belongs to its very nature; it is the unknowable. Through this dark gate (which is only a gate and not, as some theologians believe, a dwelling) the believing man steps forth into the everyday which is henceforth hallowed as the place in which he has to live with the mystery.

—Martin Buber, *The Eclipse of God*

Grace is everywhere.

—Georges Bernanos, *Diary of a Country Priest*

Traditional Prayers

ANIMA CHRISTI
Soul of Christ, sanctify me,
Body of Christ, save me,
Blood of Christ, enrapture me,
Water from the side of Christ, wash me,
Passion of Christ, strengthen me.
O good Jesus, hear me,
within your wounds hide me,
from the malicious enemy defend me,
never let me be parted from you,
at the hour of my death call me and bid me come to you,
that with your saints I may praise you for ever more.
Amen.

VENI, CREATOR SPIRITUS
Come, O Creator Spirit, come
Welcome to you, dear Friend, today
Fill all the hearts that you have made
Come, Spirit, stay

Gift that is God and Friend at hand
listening, understanding, freeing
fountain alive and fire and love
balm of our being

Finger of God, the Promised One
rich in your gifts, engracing Lord

Spirit that moves the heart and mind
to speak the word

Come, Spirit, give our senses light
come, Spirit, love us through and through
come, Spirit, heal our body's ills
refresh, renew

Rescue us from the evil one
Give us a peace that's swift and strong
You be our guide: we'll do your will
Keep clear of wrong

Through you, dear Spirit, may we know
The Father of all, the Word, the Son
strengthen our faith in you, dear Friend
come, Spirit, come

HAIL, HOLY QUEEN
Hail, holy Queen, Mother of mercy.
Hail our life, our sweetness, and our hope.
To thee do we cry, poor banished children of Eve.
To thee do we send up our sighs,
mourning and weeping in this valley of tears.
Turn then, most gracious Advocate,
thine eyes of mercy towards us
and after this our exile show unto us
the blessed fruit of thy womb, Jesus.
O clement, O loving, O sweet Virgin Mary.

AVE, MARIA
Hail Mary, full of grace. The Lord is with thee.
Blessed art thou among women
and blessed is the fruit of thy womb, Jesus.
Holy Mary, Mother of God, pray for us sinners
now and at the hour of our death.
Amen.

ST. PATRICK'S BREASTPLATE
Christ with me
Christ before me
Christ behind me
Christ within me
Christ beneath me
Christ above me
Christ at my right hand
Christ at my left hand
Christ where I shall lie
Christ where I shall sit
Christ where I shall stand
Christ in the heart of everyone who thinks of me
Christ in the mouth of everyone who speaks to me
Christ in every eye that looks on me
Christ in every ear that listens to me.

THE JESUS PRAYER
Lord Jesus Christ, Son of God, have mercy on me, a sinner.

acknowledgments & notes

ACKNOWLEDGMENTS

Grateful acknowledgment is made to the following for permission to use copyrighted material:

Biblical quotations and excerpts from the Psalms are from the *New Revised Standard Version*, copyright 1989, by the Division of Christian Education of the National Council of the Churches of Christ in the USA. Used by permission. All rights reserved.

Excerpts from the English translation of *The Roman Missal*, copyright 1973, International Committee on English in the Liturgy, Inc. All rights reserved; English translation of the *Benedictus* and *Magnificat* by the International Consultation on English Texts.

Selections from *Mystery and Manners: Occasional Prose*, Selected & Edited by Sally and Robert Fitzgerald, copyright 1957, 1961, 1963, 1966, 1967, 1969 by the Estate of Mary Flannery O'Connor, copyright 1962 by Flannery O'Connor, copyright 1961 by Farrar, Straus and Giroux, LLC; selections from *The Habit of Being*, Letters Edited and with an Introduction by Sally Fitzgerald, copyright 1979 by Regina O'Connor, introduction copyright by Sarah Fitzgerald. Published by arrangement with Farrar, Straus and Giroux, LLC. All Rights reserved.

Traditional Prayers included in the Occasions for Meditation: Prayers, Poems & Prose Passages, several of the Prayers and

Sayings of the Saints, and the poem "Lead, Kindly Light" by John Henry Newman are quoted from *Great Christian Prayers: Their History and Meaning*, by Stephen Redmond, sj (Dublin: Columba Press, 2001), and are used with permission.

The poem "Of the Divine Word" by St. John of the Cross included in the Prayers and Sayings of the Saints comes from Willis Barnstone's translation of *The Poems of St. John of the Cross* (New York: New Directions, 1972), and is used with permission.

The poems of Gerard Manley Hopkins included in the Gathering of Devotional Poems are quoted from *Gerard Manley Hopkins: The Major Works*, edited by Catherine Phillips (London: Oxford University Press, 2002), and are used by permission.

Passages by Teilhard de Chardin are quoted from *The Divine Milieu* (New York: Harper and Row, 1960) and are used by permission.

NOTES

The quotation of Emily Dickinson's poem "Some Keep the Sabbath Going to Church" (#324) in the Introduction comes from Thomas H. Johnson's *The Complete Poems of Emily Dickinson* (Boston: Little, Brown & Co., 1955), 153.

The quotation of Simone Weil in the Introduction comes from "Letter IV: Spiritual Autobiography" in *Waiting for God* (New York: HarperCollins, 2001), 31.

The poems of Gerard Manley Hopkins in the Gathering of Devotional Poems are from *Gerard Manley Hopkins: The Major Works*, ed. Catherine Phillips (London: Oxford University Press, 2002), 132, 128, 152, 183.

The poems of John Donne in the Gathering of Devotional Poems are from *John Donne's Poetry: Authoritative Texts, Criticism*, ed. A.L. Clements (New York: Norton, 1966), 94-95, 85, 93-94.

The poem by John Henry Newman in the Gathering of Devotional Poems comes from *Great Christian Prayers: Their History and Meaning*, by Stephen Redmond (Dublin: Columba Press, 2001), 87.

The quotation of St. Teresa of Avila in the Prayers and Sayings of the Saints comes from *Interior Castle*, by Teresa of Avila, trans. and ed. E. Allison Peers (New York: Doubleday, 1989), 76.

The prayer of St. Teresa of Avila in the Prayers and Sayings of the Saints comes from *Women in Praise of the Sacred*, ed. Jane Hirshfield (New York: HarperCollins, 1994), 144.

St. John of the Cross's "Of the Divine Word" included in the Prayers and Sayings of the Saints comes from Willis Barnstone's translation of *The Poems of St. John of the Cross* (New York: New Directions, 1972), 91.

The quotations from Abba Nilus and Abba Joseph in the Prose Passages come from *The Sayings of the Desert Fathers: The Alphabetical Collection,* rev. ed., trans. Benedicta Ward (Kalamazoo, Mich: Cistercian Publications, 1984), 154, xxi.

The quotations from Fyodor Dostoyevsky's *Brothers Karamozov* in the Prose Passages come from the Everyman's Library translation by Richard Pevear and Larissa Volokhonsky, (New York: Knopf,1992), 58, 319.

The quotations from Teilhard de Chardin in the Prose Passages are from *The Divine Milieu* (New York: Harper and Row, 1960), 13, 66, 86.

The quotation from Jean Guitton on Augustine in the Prose Passages comes from his *The Modernity of St. Augustine*, trans. V. Littledale (Baltimore: Helicon Press, 1959), 16.

The quotation from Claude Tresmontant in the Prose Passages comes from his *A Study of Hebrew Thought*, trans. Michael Francis Gibson (New York: Desclee Company, 1960), 153.

The quotation from Martin Buber in the Prose Passages comes from his *The Eclipse of God: Studies in the Relation between Religion and Philosophy* (New York: Harper and Row, 1957), 36.

The quotation from Georges Bernanos's *Diary of a Country Priest* is from Pamela Morris's translation of the novel (New York: Carroll & Graf, 1965), 298.

The Traditional Prayers and the Prayers and Sayings of the Saints (with the exception of those by St. Teresa of Avila and St. John of the Cross) are quoted from Stephen Redmond's *Great Christian Prayers: Their History and Meaning* (Dublin: Columba Press, 2001), 19, 53, 55, 59, 63, 71, 75, 77, 81, 83.

PERSONAL ACKNOWLEDGMENTS

I am very grateful to friends and colleagues who have assisted me in completing this book. First, my thanks must go to editors Lil Copan and Paul Elie, for inviting me to create a book of hours based on Flanney O'Connor's prayer life. In addition, I am grateful to my colleagues at Fordham University's Curran Center for American Catholic Studies. To Richard Giannone, whose contributions to O'Connor scholarship are without parallel, I am grateful for inspiration, conversation about the project, and encouragement. To Mark Massa, SJ, Christine Firer Hinze, and Maria Terzulli, I am grateful for their enthusiasm about this book and for their patience and support during the long process of preparing this manuscript. And to our student workers, Ileana Beatances, Jenny Portillo, and Paul Schutz, I am grateful for their dedication to running our center with ease and grace, thus allowing me hours to devote to this book of hours. I am also grateful to my students in the American Catholic Studies Program, whose engagement of O'Connor's work in the classroom is characteristically enthusiastic, energetic, and inspirational.

Finally, I would like to thank my family—my husband, Brennan, and our three sons, Charles, Patrick, and Will—for their patience during the course of this project, their kindness in listening to me think aloud about Flannery O'Connor on a daily basis, and their willingness to read portions of the book and offer helpful responses. These men are great blessings in my life, whose presence takes me, daily, to the Province of Joy. This book is dedicated to them.

About Paraclete Press

You May Also Be Interested In . . .

Shirt of Flame
A YEAR WITH ST. THÉRÈSE OF LISIEUX

Heather King

ISBN: 978-1-55725-808-3
$16.99, French Flap

"This book brings out the grit of sanctity, how it is a continuous, no-holds-barred, full-on contact engagement with reality. The episodes from St. Thérèse's life and Ms. King's reflections concerning her own path show how both the French Carmelite and the her L.A.-based follower simplify their lives, not as an escape, but precisely in order to face without distraction the gargantuan challenge and adventure of love, surrender, living out, to the last drop, their embrace of the Savior of the world."

—*Fr. Vincent T. Nagle, Holy Family Parish, Ramallah, West Bank,
The Palestinian Territories*

At the Still Point
A LITERARY GUIDE TO PRAYER IN ORDINARY TIME

Sarah Arthur

ISBN: 978-1-55725-785-7
$16.99, Trade paperback

"What a delight to find so extraordinary a collection meant for use in ordinary time! Any book that includes passages from *The Wind in the Willows* and *Moby Dick*, as well as poems by George Herbert and Christina Rossetti, is all right with me . . . each of the works chosen is meant to awaken me to the movement of the spirit in daily life." —*Kathleen Norris, author of* Dakota *and* Cloister Walk

*Available from most booksellers or through Paraclete Press:
www.paracletepress.com; 1-800-451-5006. Try your local bookstore first.*